全国高等教育商务英语规划系列教材

商务英语阅读
Business English Reading

主　编　金焕荣
副主编　吴建国　陈　羔
编　者　金焕荣　季甜甜
　　　　刘　萱　季　宇

苏州大学出版社

图书在版编目(CIP)数据

商务英语阅读=Business English Reading / 金焕荣主编. —苏州:苏州大学出版社,2022.1
全国高等教育商务英语规划系列教材
ISBN 978-7-5672-3817-6

Ⅰ.①商… Ⅱ.①金… Ⅲ.①商务-英语-阅读教学-高等学校-教材 Ⅳ.①F7

中国版本图书馆 CIP 数据核字(2022)第 001629 号

书　　名:	商务英语阅读 Business English Reading
主　　编:	金焕荣
策划编辑:	汤定军
责任编辑:	汤定军
装帧设计:	吴　钰
出版发行:	苏州大学出版社(Soochow University Press)
社　　址:	苏州市十梓街1号　邮编:215006
印　　刷:	江苏凤凰数码印务有限公司
邮购热线:	0512-67480030
销售热线:	0512-67481020
开　　本:	787 mm×1 092 mm　1/16　印张:10　字数:237千
版　　次:	2022年1月第1版
印　　次:	2022年1月第1次印刷
书　　号:	ISBN 978-7-5672-3817-6
定　　价:	35.00元

凡购本社图书发现印装错误,请与本社联系调换。服务热线:0512-67481020
苏州大学出版社营销部　电话:0512-67481020
苏州大学出版社网址　http://www.sudapress.com
苏州大学出版社邮箱　sdcbs@suda.edu.cn

全国高等教育商务英语规划系列教材

顾　问　　徐青根　　鲁加升

编　委　　（以姓氏笔画为序）

于延梅	王红华	王金华	王　娅
王　翔	王德丽	毛卫强	方小勇
文　格	朱冬梅	刘　萱	孙亚玲
孙志祥	李卫东	步阳辉	季甜甜
季　宇	张　莹	张夏菲	张　涛
陈东东	陈　羔	陈　培	林又佳
杨　晓	金焕荣	郑　骏	顾　红
顾秀梅	顾　薇	袁海燕	施　翔
姚春宁	姚菊霞	徐　健	徐　源
程进军	曾　艳	潘　珺	穆连涛

策　划　　汤定军

编者的话

21世纪的中国，改革开放不断深化，对外经济交往愈加频繁。在经济全球化的大背景下，许多外国企业相继来华投资，我国许多企业也力争打入国际市场，以谋求更大的发展。目前，我国的对外经济交流已发展到对外贸易、对外投资、对外经济技术合作等多个领域。因此，日益广泛的国际商务领域对国际商务英语人才的培养在数量上和质量上都提出了新的要求。而随着许多涉外用人单位对精通商务英语的求职者的青睐，一个学习商务英语的热潮正悄然而起。编写一本与时俱进且普遍适用的商务英语阅读教程，以适应社会主义市场经济发展的要求，是我们携手编写此书的初衷。商务英语阅读是在对外贸易、对外交流等活动中的一项重要技能。这套教材重在培养既有扎实的英语语言功底，又有丰富的经贸知识，并能在商务实践中灵活自如地应对各种场面的复合型人才。

选稿之初，编者从两个角度出发，一方面考虑教材的时代性，力求内容新颖，与时俱进；另一方面考虑教材的实用性和科学性，争取涉及广泛，适合阅读，扩大读者的知识面以及词汇量。在选稿过程中，编者严格依照以上两个出发点，经过多重考虑，层层筛选，最终选定的文章不仅内容新颖，在相关领域具有代表性，而且篇章完整，有词汇及短语、阅读理解、段落翻译以及讨论话题。这些文章大多出自近年来国内外出版的专著、知名报刊，内容涉及经济、贸易、金融、投资、管理、环境、商务文化、电子商务、旅游等多个方面。各类学习者通过学习本教材，不仅可以扩大国际商务知识面，而且能够切实提高阅读能力。

在编写过程中，我们参阅了国内外出版的大量有关资料和信息。主要参考文献目录附于书末。在此，谨表诚挚的谢意。

由于编者经验不足、水平有限，错漏之处在所难免，恳请学界同仁和读者不吝赐教。

金焕荣
2021 年 10 月

使用说明

本书可用作英语专业研究生、本科生以及通过国家英语等级考试的经济、贸易、管理等相关专业学生的自学教材或专业英语教材，还可供企业在职人员培训时使用以及有志于从事国际商务活动的人士自学之用。

本书共由 36 个单元组成，每单元均由正文、词汇及短语、阅读理解、段落翻译和话题讨论 5 个部分组成。正文（Passage）大多出自近年来国内外出版的专著、知名报刊，内容涉及经济、贸易、金融、投资、管理、环境、商务文化、电子商务、旅游等多个方面；词汇及短语（Words and Expressions）针对上下文语境给出单词及词组的解释；阅读理解（Comprehension）通过问题帮助读者加深对课文的理解；段落翻译（Translation）则是在培养读者阅读能力的同时，提高其翻译和表达能力；话题讨论（Questions for Discussion）针对课文内容，结合当前时事给出话题，有助于培养读者的思考能力，扩大读者的知识面。

本书用作全日制学生的教材时，建议一周开设 4 个课时，每两个课时讲解 1 个单元，每周讲解 2 个单元，一学期可将全书内容讲解完毕。此外，文章选材难易程度不同，教师可酌情选取，自行安排讲解顺序。

金焕荣
2021 年 10 月

Contents

Unit 1	Getting to "Yes" with the Business Plan (I)	1
Unit 2	Getting to "Yes" with the Business Plan (II)	5
Unit 3	Why Do Businesses Need Funds?	10
Unit 4	Balancing Act	14
Unit 5	A Sharp AIM	17
Unit 6	Shattered Faith	20
Unit 7	China's Unwelcome Mat	23
Unit 8	The Key Challenges Facing Corporate America at Present	27
Unit 9	The Management Process	32
Unit 10	China Must Slow Down a Bit	37
Unit 11	Changes and Challenges	40
Unit 12	Can Asia-Pacific Go the EU Way?	44
Unit 13	Economic Growth Promotes Regional Financial Cooperation in Asia	47
Unit 14	How Higher Oil Prices Affect the Global Economy	51
Unit 15	Waste Not Want Not	55
Unit 16	Those Gloating Dismal Scientists	59
Unit 17	Five Steps to Prevent Future Energy Woes	62

Unit 18	Green or Gray?	66
Unit 19	Recycling Big	70
Unit 20	Forex Rate Forming Mechanism Reformed	73
Unit 21	Money Supply Target Lowered	76
Unit 22	Strategy in the Knowledge Economy	79
Unit 23	The Communication Advantage	84
Unit 24	The Revolution in Risk Management	89
Unit 25	The Risk of Liberalization and Its Solution	94
Unit 26	The Value of Being in Control	98
Unit 27	Work beyond 2010	104
Unit 28	What's Hot on the Cyberspace Hit List	110
Unit 29	To Be a Well-off Witkey?	114
Unit 30	Virtual World, Real Fortune	117
Unit 31	Hanging by a Thread	122
Unit 32	Spam, to Go	125
Unit 33	Google Gooses Big Media	129
Unit 34	The Meat and Potatoes of Culture	133
Unit 35	Money Speaks	136
Unit 36	Competitive Travel	139
Vocabulary		142

Passage

Getting to "Yes" with the Business Plan (Ⅰ)
Joe Tabet & Albert Angehrn

Competition for venture capital is fierce and investors look hard at web start-ups, making a good business plan essential. **Joe Tabet** and **Albert Angehrn** offer their advice.

Joe Tabet is adjunct professor of entrepreneurship at Insead and senior vice president of business creation at Gorilla Park.

Albert Angehrn is professor of information technology and entrepreneurship, and director of the Center for Advanced Learning Technologies at Insead.

The new economy has revolutionized the way we are doing business and the businesses are created. Underlying the changes is the way venture capital has made it possible to finance an idea or a team even before there is any product or patent. In 1999, "gold rush entrepreneurship" flourished and was fed by an abundance of funding. However, the times when anyone could get financed are over; investors are looking for well-structured, credible projects. Negative sentiment to Internet start-ups means e-business plans need to be at least as solid as traditional business plans.

This article aims to help entrepreneurs wanting to start a business. The objective is not to provide a template for a business plan, but to give hints, based on the experience of those who have already done it, be they entrepreneurs or investors. Writing a business plan develops understanding and provides a focus on the essentials. It may seem a time-consuming, even painful, exercise, but the returns are worth the effort.

Structure

The business plan summarizes a project in a way that makes it understandable and attractive to potential investors, business partners, or employees. It should contain a clear message for the target audience and has to be tailored, in the same way that a curriculum vitae needs to be modified to match each job position. The business plan has three objectives:

- To give a clear, understandable description of the opportunity.

- To provide convincing arguments that make the opportunity credible.
- To formulate a direct request to investors, strategic partners, or potential employees.

Box 1   Facts and Figures

● A respectable venture capital company receives 100 to 150 business plans to consider each month.
● Only 0.3 percent to 1 percent of business plans get funded.
● Despite the fact that the most common case of failure of e-businesses is the lack of market acceptance, only 3 percent of business plans give meaningful evidence of customer acceptance.
● Roughly 40 percent of business plans contain an extensive competition analysis.

Keep in mind that the first review of a business plan is an elimination process, rather than a selection process. The challenge is to stimulate readers' curiosity and allow them to read the plan easily. Venture capital companies have to go through many proposals, all competing for the same money; you miss out important details at your peril (see Box 1). The objective should be to get an invitation to make a detailed presentation, which is the real selection process.

Three types of documents should be prepared: an "elevator pitch", an executive summary, and the business plan. The elevator pitch is a one-paragraph description of the business, presented as if you were in an elevator with an investor. You would have 30 seconds to stimulate interest. The pitch can be printed on a business card or a flyer. The executive summary is what readers should remember. It should be no longer than four pages and can be sent to initial contracts. Finally, the business plan gives the details in no more than 20 pages, or 30 slides for a presentation. Longer documents force readers to make their own selection, which may not be your favor. It is more difficult to write a short document than a long one. By getting to the essentials, you will gain a better understanding of the important issues.

Contents

The business plan should start with a clear value proposition. What matters to the reader is the value your business will create. A clear value proposition will answer the following:

- What kind of business are you in?
- What do you provide and how?
- Who are your target customers?

The plan should clearly identify the problem, not only the solution. Many projects are too solution-driven; success resides in a good understanding of the problem. First confirm the need, and then build the product. Show you understand the problem and your solution will be more convincing.

Be focused. With an e-business plan, it is no longer necessary to point out that the number of internet users will be growing exponentially and that the market will be worth billions in 2005. Avoid industry description and focus on the business. Define the target market and provide a relevant description, with figures that show the size of the market. Projects that bet on capturing a small fraction of a huge market, which may in theory represent billions, are unlikely to fly. If this principle worked, "we should all be selling tea in China."

Highlight the "so what". If you want readers to reach your conclusions, rather than their own, you need to steer them. It is not enough to describe facts. Different readers may draw different conclusions. For example, the fact that some people don't wear shoes doesn't indicate whether there is a huge potential market for shoes or no market at all.

Show some evidence of market acceptance, in particular with a new product or concept. Consumer behavior is hard to predict. A common pitfall is to assume customers will behave in the way you expect. Reality is different and common sense is the least accurate way to predict people's attitudes.

Describe the implementation approach. A good idea is unlikely to be unique. If it's good, expect a few other people to be thinking about it. If it's really good, you may find others working on it already. The difference is in execution. This is the real challenge. Even if the idea is not unique, you can make a difference in the way you implement it—this is what investors are looking for.

Be coherent with figures. There will never be accurate figures until the business is underway and even then some pieces may be missing. However, it is always possible to use comparisons, benchmarks, and reference points. Use them to estimate market size, market share, and profit margins. Unless you really miss the point, you should be much better positioned than anyone else to find the best figures. If it is difficult to find estimates, potential investors are even less likely to find better estimates.

At first, investors will not be able to check the figures. They would rather look at the coherence of figures and check that they are consistent with the strategy. If a key factor for success is to reach critical mass rapidly, focus on customer acquisition and put in the resources up front to do that. A timid approach, taking a percentage of revenue for marketing, is unlikely to match a jump-start strategy.

Words & Expressions

start-up	n.	the act of starting a new operation or practice
adjunct	n.	a person who is an assistant or subordinate to another
template	n.	a model or standard for making comparisons
curriculum vitae		a summary of your academic and work history; resume

elimination	n.	analysis of a problem into alternative possibilities followed by the systematic rejection of unacceptable alternatives
pitch	n.	promotion by means of an argument and demonstration
proposition	n.	an unproved statement in which an opinion or judgment is expressed
reside	vi.	to belong to
exponentially	adv.	in an exponential manner
capture	vt.	to succeed in catching or seizing, especially after a chase
pitfall	n.	an unforeseen or unexpected or surprising difficulty

Comprehension

1. Why is a good business plan essential? And what are the objectives of a business plan?
2. What have you got from Box 1?
3. What does "elevator pitch" mean? And what's the advantage of it?
4. What can be called a clear value proposition?
5. What do the contents of a good business plan require?

Translation

Please translate the part in waves into Chinese.

Questions for Discussion

1. Say what you know about venture capital.
2. What are essential factors for business start-ups?

Passage

Getting to "Yes" with the Business Plan (II)
Joe Tabet & Albert Angehrn

The Format

Use an easy-to-read format, be creative in composing the document, but don't go to extremes. Find a balance: complicated documents are irritating and flat text with long paragraphs is boring. Think about the way people read a newspaper: they check the headlines first and focus on interesting stories. Readers of business plans are not different. They like catchy titles, tend to read in diagonals, and have a short attention span. So, make it easy to get the essentials. Use margins for quotes or comments and appropriate graphics. End with the points you want people to remember.

Don't use small type and never exceed 30 pages, including appendices. If readers want more, they can ask; if they want less, they don't know what to leave out. Keep in mind that the file may have to be sent by e-mail. Large files take time to download, particularly in hotel rooms.

What to Include

Use a simple style, common vocabulary, and avoid abbreviations. Use analogies, without being too vague. (For example, don't say you want to be the Amazon for Africa.) Describe the business in a way that makes it easy to understand. It is not enough to say you want to build a reference portal for mobile phone users; you may need to explain what your business is about and how you will be doing it. As a general rule, start with the "most important", then go to the details and finally go back to the important again.

Business Description

First, describe the need to be addressed and the market opportunity it represents. Next, explain how this need will be met. Then show how you want to implement the idea, the business approach. Illustrate the product or service with examples. Use customer scenarios or storyboards to explain how it will work. Always take the client's perspective and never expect them to do something you wouldn't.

Team and Organization

Draw the organization chart as it should be at maturity, not to fit the current team. Highlight the team's capabilities and don't hesitate to identify gaps. This shows awareness of future needs. Mention the strategy for recruiting other key people and the top executives who are willing to join the team once financing is found. (However, this may not be taken seriously because it doesn't show commitment.)

An advisory board adds credibility, in particular if it is composed of well-known experts. Nevertheless, be careful with name dropping: the world is small and serious investors are diligent. In summary, show the competencies you already have, but stay realistic, humble, and credible.

Your team is your most valuable asset; choose people very carefully. They will determine the success of the business. The team is the first element investors look at.

Competitive Analysis

It is a mistake not to include a thorough analysis of potential competition. If there is no direct competitor, look for alternatives or substitutes for the product. If there is no competition it is not necessarily a positive point; in fact it may be very negative, because there is no market for the idea.

Once competition has been covered, show the differentiating points. Avoid the line of "better, cheaper, and faster". Keep in mind that what you see of existing competition is only the tip of the iceberg. If two companies are offering a similar service, there are probably a dozen preparing to launch. Also take into consideration the schedule competitors may be following. For example, if you want to offer features that competitors are not offering, but it will take six months before you start up, competitors—particularly on the web—might by then have added those features.

Don't underestimate competitors' ability to catch up and don't forget bricks-and-mortar companies moving online. Geographic barriers are not always high, but they have to be taken seriously if the business has multinational ambitions. Scheduling needs care; if your ambition is to cover several countries, speed is vital. If you aim to launch in one country in the first year, another two countries in the second year, and arrive in the next three large markets in the third year, it will be difficult convincing investors that the final markets will wait. Just think about the web three years ago and the speed at which applications are transferred.

Marketing Strategy

Marketing and sales are strategic components of any business. Focus on how this will be done and remember that the marketing approach may provide a competitive advantage. It has to match strategy and objectives. If the business relies on building a critical mass of customers, initial investment in client acquisition should be a priority.

Estimate marketing costs in terms of the costs of customer acquisition, rather than fixed budgets or percentage of revenues. Use reference points and comparisons to estimate the average cost of acquiring a new customer in your business category.

Implementation and Logistics

The most important determination for success is the ability to execute. Implementation is the real differentiator. This includes all aspects, from the choice of technology to customer service. On the web, first-mover advantage has proved to be insufficient to dominate the market. The game is about speed and scalability. The first one to scale up is most likely to keep the competitive edge.

As e-businesses become more independent, it is vital to find a place in the industry value chain. Strategic alliances are critical and can be very valuable at an early stage. With a smart approach, possible competitors can turn into allies or collaborators.

Evaluating the Business

Attributing value to a young business is not easy. The variability is very wide and methods used by investors keep on changing. Traditional ratios are in most cases impossible to calculate. The use of comparisons often helps. Evaluation can still be very difficult, in particular for novel applications. At a later stage, profit making will be the bottom line and traditional methods become much easier to apply. At the idea stage, venture capitalists tend to use very simple formulae to evaluate potential, such as:

Potential = market size × market growth × your contribution

No matter what the valuation is, think of the business as a way of creating assets. The assets can be anything that contributes to the value of the company. Influence the choice of valuation method by defining some measurable assets that can be used. Assets are always a mix of tangible and intangible, such as goodwill or brand name, or human capital and intellectual property. A customer (or supplier) base can also represent a measurable asset. In choosing a particular asset, make sure your implementation gives absolute priority to maximizing this asset's value and how to measure it.

As a general guideline for early-stage valuation, here are some rules:
- An idea is worth nothing if it remains an idea.
- Nothing can be protected, even with a million patents.
- Take the money when it's available; windows of opportunity are narrow.
- All evaluation methods are good; none makes sense.

- Time is money; don't waste it on negotiation.
- Focus on the investors' value-added and not on valuation.

Always include a section analyzing the risks that may affect the business. An accurate assessment of risks will help convince investors that you are fully aware of the threats the business may face. It also shows that you are prepared and capable of responding to the challenge.

Don't forget to state clearly what is expected from the target audience. The conclusion should include your funding request. You can also include a bullet-point summary to help the readers find what they have to take away. Remember, attention span is short, retention is low, and the memory decay curve is steep.

Conclusion
- Use the business plan as a communication tool.
- Be simple, realistic, and use common sense.
- Don't look for funding, but for raising interest.
- At the first stage, success is to get to the second round.
- Be ready to support any statement with detailed information.

Words & Expressions

catchy	adj.	likely to attract attention
diagonal	n.	a straight line that joins two opposite sides of sth. at an angle; a straight line that is at an angle
scenario	n.	a postulated sequence of possible events
substitute	n.	a person or thing that takes or can take the place of another
underestimate	vt.	to make too low an estimate of
scalability	n.	the quality of being scalable
alliance	n.	an organization of people (or countries) involved in a pact or treaty
retention	n.	the power of retaining and recalling past experience

Comprehension
1. What's the proper format of a business plan? And why?
2. How do you make a business description?
3. What is the first element investors look at? And how to describe it well?
4. Is it necessary to include a thorough analysis of potential competition in a business plan? And why?
5. According to the article, what are the rules for early-stage valuation of a business?

Translation
Please translate the parts in waves into Chinese.

Questions for Discussion
1. Talk about how to write a good business plan.
2. Discuss possible ways of raising funds for a business idea.

Unit 3

Passage

Why Do Businesses Need Funds?
Ricky W. Griffin & Ronald J. Ebert

Every company must spend money to survive: according to the simplest formula, funds that are spent on materials, wages, and buildings eventually lead to the creation of products, revenues, and profits. In planning for funding requirements, financial managers must distinguish between two different kinds of expenditures: short-term (operating) and long-term (capital) expenditures.

Short-term (Operating) Expenditures

Short-term expenditures are incurred regularly in a firm's everyday business activities. To manage these outlays, managers must pay special attention to accounts payable, accounts receivable, and inventories. We will also describe the measures used by some firms in managing the funds known as working capital.

Accounts Payable

Previously we defined accounts payable as unpaid bills owed to suppliers plus wages and taxes due within the upcoming year. For most companies, this is the largest single category of short-term debt. To plan for funding flows, financial managers want to know in advance the amounts of new accounts payable as well as when they must be repaid. For information about such obligations and needs—for example, the quantity of supplies required by a certain department in an upcoming period—financial managers must rely on other managers.

Accounts Receivable

As we described before, accounts receivable consist of funds due from customers who have bought on credit. A sound financial plan requires financial managers to project accurately both how much and when buyers will make payments on these accounts. Managers at Kraft Foods must know how many dollars' worth of cheddar cheese Kroger's supermarkets will order each month; they must also know Kroger's payment schedule. Because they represent an investment in products for which a firm has not yet received payment, accounts receivable temporarily tie up its funds. Clearly, the seller wants to receive payment as quickly as possible.

Credit Policies

Predicting payment schedules is a function of credit policy: the rules governing a firm's extension of credit to customers. This policy sets standards as to which buyers are eligible for what type of credit. Typically, credit is extended to customers who have the ability to pay and who honor their obligations. Credit is denied to firms with poor payment histories. Information about such histories is available from many sources, including the Credit Interchange developed by the National Association of Credit Management.

Credit policy also sets payment terms. For example, credit terms "2/10", "net 30" mean that the selling company offers a 2% discount if the customer pays within 10 days and the customer has 30 days to pay the regular price. Under these terms, the buyer would have to pay only $980 on a $1,000 invoice on days 1 to 10, but all $1,000 on days 11 to 30. The higher the discount, the more incentive buyers have to pay early. Sellers can thus adjust credit terms to influence when customers pay their bills.

Inventories

Between the time a firm buys raw materials and the time it sells finished products, it ties up funds in inventory—materials and goods that it will sell within the year. There are three basic types of inventories:

- The supplies that a firm purchases for use in production are its raw materials inventory. Raw materials inventory at Lee Apparel Co. includes huge rolls of denim.
- Work-in-process inventory consists of goods that have moved partway through the production process. Thus, jeans that have been cut out but not yet sewn are work-in-process inventory at Lee.
- Finished-goods inventory consists of items ready for sale. Completed blue jeans ready for shipment to dealers are part of Lee's finished-goods inventory.

Failure to manage inventory can have grave financial consequences. Too little inventory of any kind can cost a firm sales. Too much inventory mean tied-up funds that cannot be used elsewhere. In extreme cases, a company may have to sell excess inventory at low profits simply to raise cash.

Working Capital

Basically, working capital consists of a firm's current assets on hand. It is a liquid asset out of which current debts can be paid. A company calculates its working capital by adding up the following:

Inventories—that is, raw materials, work-in-process, and finished goods on hand.

Accounts receivable (minus accounts payable).

How much money is tied up in working capital? Fortune 500 companies typically devote 20 cents of every sales dollar—about $1.2 trillion total—to working capital. What are the benefits of reducing these sums? There are two very important pluses:

1. Every dollar that is not tied up in working capital becomes a dollar of more useful cash flow.

2. Reduction of working capital raises earnings permanently.

The second advantage results from the fact that money costs money (in interest payments and the like). Reducing working capital, therefore, means saving money.

Long-term (Capital) Expenditures

In addition to needing funds for operating expenditures, companies need funds to cover long-term expenditures on fixed assets. Fixed assets are items with long-term use or value, such as land, buildings, and machinery.

Long-term expenditures are usually more carefully planned than short-term outlays because they pose special problems. They differ from short-term outlays in the following ways, all of which influence the ways that long-term outlays are funded:

- Unlike inventories and other short-term assets, they are not normally sold or converted into cash.
- Their acquisition requires a very large investment.
- They represent a binding commitment of company funds that continues long into the future.

Words & Expressions

incur	vt.	to make oneself subject to; bring upon oneself; become liable to; receive a specified treatment (abstract)
outlay	n.	money paid out or expenditure
working capital		liquid current assets out of which a firm can pay current debts
buy on credit		to buy something in a way that payment will be done later
project	vt.	to make or work out a plan for
tie up		to restrain from moving or operating normally
credit policy		rules governing a firm's extension of credit to customers

honor	vt.	to accept as pay; show respect towards; abide by
inventory	n.	materials and goods that are held by a company but will be sold within the year
convert	vt.	to obtain an equivalent value for in an exchange or calculation, as money or units of measurement

Comprehension
1. How do short-term and long-term expenditures differ from each other?
2. What does a sound financial plan require?
3. What're the functions of credit policies?
4. How many basic types of inventories are there? What are they?
5. What are the benefits of reducing working capital? And why?

Translation
Please translate the parts in waves into Chinese.

Questions for Discussion
1. Say what you know about the sources of short-term financing for business.
2. Say what you know about the sources of long-term financing for business and the risks entailed by each type.

Unit 4

Passage

Balancing Act
Raghuram Rajan

Asia's dynamism has reshaped the global economic landscape, and the IMF is trying to adapt.

The International Monetary Fund (IMF) is holding its annual meeting in Southeast Asia this week. Nearly ten years have passed since the 1997 Asian crisis, so this is an anniversary of sorts—a not entirely happy one. The IMF's image in Asia suffered from perceived missteps it made during the crisis. Yet the fund also did a lot right (as was shown by the region's rapid recovery), and since the crisis the IMF has changed. More changes are in the works. At the meeting in Singapore, the fund is pursuing reforms that will give greater influence to emerging economic powers in Asia and elsewhere. The IMF is also taking steps that address some of the misgivings about the way it has worked in the past to prevent and resolve financial turmoil.

Some background: one of the IMF's primary missions is to be an emergency lender to countries suffering from economic shocks, such as sudden currency devaluation. During the Asian crisis, the IMF loaned billions of dollars to countries including Thailand, Indonesia and South Korea, where years of excessive borrowing and frenzied investment by a financially overstretched private sector (abetted by errant government policies) led to sharp economic reversals. While IMF intervention helped put those countries on the road to recovery, it was not without controversy. For example, the IMF initially urged governments to cut spending, but quickly reversed itself when it saw this would further slow damaged economies. The prevailing Asian view then was that as a condition for receiving assistance, the IMF pushed Asian governments to adopt policies that furthered the interests of industrialized nations, the IMF's largest shareholders.

Determined never to be at the mercy of foreigners again, many Asian countries have since built up huge foreign-exchange reserves as a buffer against financial shocks. Emerging Asia now has currency reserves approaching $2 trillion. Self-insured against everything short of Armageddon, these nations have little incentive to engage in discussions about the international financial system, but the world needs such dialogue more than ever. There are risks to the global economy posed by mounting trade imbalances, especially the US's huge trade deficit (around 6% of GDP) and the soaring surpluses in emerging Asia, some European economies, and oil-producing nations. These imbalances cannot be mitigated by the Group of Seven (G-7) industrial countries alone. The fact is, the global economy is very different from what it was 20 years ago, when the G-7 accounted for half the world's GDP measured in purchasing-power parity. Then, large industrial economies had little need to consult the rest of the world. Today, the six largest economies outside the G-7—including Brazil, China, India and Russia—now account for 30% of global GDP. Yet China, despite its economic heft, has fewer votes at the IMF than any of the G-7 nations.

Dynamic emerging economies need a greater role in managing the global economy. The IMF has set up a mechanism, called multilateral consultations, designed to bring together groups that are economically large enough to resolve common problems while being numerically small enough to engage in candid discussion. Depending on the problem, the group will vary—for example, the first multilateral consultation brings together China, the Euro area, Japan, Saudi Arabia and the US to discuss how to narrow global trade imbalances.

The IMF is also changing the way it lends. Emerging markets remain vulnerable to financial-market turbulence—we saw a mild version of this in May. Not only is it costly, however, for a country to build its foreign reserves to protect against such risks, it also hurts the global economy if the country holds down its exchange rate in order to export more to build those reserves. There needs to be an alternative, an IMF lending facility that provides assurance to countries that financing will be available if, despite sound policies, they are hit by turbulence—and that this funding will not have onerous conditions attached by the IMF, conditions that were so resented during the Asia crisis. The precise structure of such a facility is currently being debated by the fund and its members.

Finally, for the IMF to be seen by all its members as a legitimate place for multilateral dialogue, and for them to trust the fund as a lender, members must feel adequately represented. A central focus of reform today is the restructuring of voting power to better reflect changes in economic importance, as well as to give small poor countries more of a say. This is no easy task. A gain for some will mean a loss for others. But if reforms enacted in Singapore bolster confidence in the IMF, everybody wins—and future anniversaries should be happy affairs.

Words & Expressions

misstep	n.	an instance of wrong or improper conduct; a blunder
misgiving	n.	a feeling of doubt, distrust, or apprehension
frenzied	adj.	widely excited or agitated; frantic
abet	vt.	to approve, encourage, and support (an action or a plan of action); urge and help on
buffer	n.	something that lessens or absorbs the shock of an impact
mounting	adj.	increasing
mitigate	vt.	to moderate (a quality or condition) in force or intensity; alleviate
heft	n.	importance; influence
onerous	adj.	needing effort; burdensome
enact	vt.	to ordain; decree
bolster	vt.	to give support to sb./sth.; strengthen or reinforce sth.

Comprehension

1. Why did the IMF need to change after the crisis? Can you illustrate briefly how it has changed?
2. Is it true or false that the author believes it was without controversy while the IMF intervention helped put those crisis-attacked Asian countries on the road to recovery?
3. Does the author think much of many Asian countries' practice of building up huge foreign-exchange reserves as a buffer against financial shocks?
4. Why does the author say the global economy is very different from what it was 20 years ago?
5. What is the central focus of reform?

Translation
Please translate the part in waves into Chinese.

Questions for Discussion
1. How much do you know about the 1997 Asian crisis?
2. What kind of role do IMF and WB play in the global economy respectively?

Passage

A Sharp AIM
Adam Smith

Small firms are flooding London's Alternative Investment Market. Is it smart to let so many of them in?

Like many 5-year-olds, California's Vycon corporation is going through a growth spurt. A developer of mechanical energy-storage devices (essentially batteries made of flywheels rather than chemicals), the firm is beefing up production of some of its gadgets tenfold this year to quench demand. To pay for such expansion, Vycon's executives decided to sell shares to the public. Too tiny to trade on New York City's NASDAQ, the company focused instead on another market catering to ambitious upstarts like Vycon. "London's Alternatives Investment Market (AIM) was a global market for small companies," says Vycon president and CEO Tony Aoun, which would "put the company in a good light". When the business was listed on AIM in March, investors poured in $18 million, fulfilling Vycon's best hopes.

London's dramatic renaissance as perhaps the world's leading financial center has been a well-documented phenomenon in recent years. But relatively little attention has been paid to just how important AIM has been to that resurgence. Launched by the London Stock Exchange (LSE) in 1995, AIM now lists more than 1,600 companies, five times the number of a decade ago. Turnover in its shares hit $114 billion in 2006, some way from the $3.8 billion bartered in its first full year. AIM attracted 198 initial public offerings last year, four times the number on the LSE's main market, and considerably more than on the New York Stock Exchange (NYSE) or NASDAQ.

AIM offers companies seeking capital a chance to dip into London's deep investor pool under lighter regulations than those on competing markets. That's got US rivals in a spin. As overseas firms bypass New York to trade on AIM—which now lists more than 300 foreign companies, one-fifth of them from the US—it has faced accusations of lax standards. In January, NYSE CEO John Thain claimed AIM "did not have any standards at all, and anyone could list." A month later, Roel Campos, a commissioner at the US Securities and Exchange Commission, the stock-market regulator, branded AIM a "casino", with 30% of new firms "gone in a year". (He later said his remarks had been taken out of context.) To the LSE, such talk is just sour grapes. US markets should accept that "the flow of capital is global and will seek out the most efficient and effective market places," Clara Furse, the exchange's chief, wrote in the *Financial Times* in late March.

AIM's way of vetting companies is hardly traditional. To float on the LSE's main market, a company normally needs a three-year business record, a minimum market cap and shareholder approval for big acquisitions or disposals; NASDAQ and NYSE have similar hurdles. But AIM's quality control is outsourced to 85 so-called Nominated Advisers, or Nomads. Generally accounting firms or financial management companies, Nomads scrutinize a firm's executive staff, business model and performance before deciding whether it can list. To a degree, NYSE's Thain is right: AIM has very few prescriptive requirements for listing—the Nomad's own judgment is key.

Since the Nomad's fees are paid for by the company wanting to be listed, it might seem that AIM is built on a giant conflict of interest, but Nomads counter that traditional auditors and accountants are company-paid, too. In practice, says Philip Secrett, a partner at Grant Thornton Corporate Finance, one of the largest Nomads, only a "small minority" progress onto AIM; most are turned away for being too immature or unsound. And there is AIM's track record: around 3% of AIM-listed companies fail annually, a figure roughly comparable with the main market.

AIM's advocates also say it strengthens regulations when warranted. Ernst & Young's index of AIM's oil and gas companies—around 7% of AIM's list—slid by 6% in 2006, a lingering reverberation from a series of shock announcements from energy firms that their reserves were dry. Last year the LSE began requesting such firms submit independent annual reports on their reserves.

But across other AIM sectors, assessing overseas businesses from London can be like drilling for oil with a blindfold. That risk is particularly acute in emerging-markets companies. "The best way to test for integrity is to ask around," says Simon Cawkwell, an independent trader who's invested millions in AIM since its launch. But, he adds, "You can't ask around in China."

Still, many AIM participants say only so much risk can be regulated out of the system. "AIM is still a stock picker's market," says Nick Bayley, head of trading services at the LSE. "This isn't a market for widows and orphans." Investors prepared to do their homework are bullish. "The prospects for AIM look as good or better than they've ever looked," says Patrick Evershed, a fund manager at New Star Asset Management in London. Vycon's Aoun encourages firms to consider AIM, but with a caveat. "This is no minor undertaking," he says. "Be ready for some serious work." After all, growing up is hard to do.

Words & Expressions

spurt	n.	a sudden increase in speed, effort, activity or emotion for a short period of time
beef up		to make sth. bigger, better, more interesting, etc.
quench	vt.	to satisfy
upstart	n.	a person who has just started in a new position or job but who behaves as if they are more important than other people, in a way that is annoying
resurgence	n.	the return and growth of an activity that had stopped
barter	vt.	to exchange
lax	adj.	not strict, severe or careful enough about work, rules or standards of behavior
vet	vt.	to check the contents, quality, etc. of sth. carefully
hurdle	n.	a problem or difficulty that must be solved or dealt with before you can achieve sth.
reverberation	n.	the effects of sth. that happens, especially unpleasant ones that spread among a large number of people
caveat	n.	a warning that particular things need to be considered before sth. can be done

Comprehension

1. Why did Vycon trade on AIM?
2. Describe briefly the development of AIM in recent years.
3. Please compare AIM's way of vetting companies with that of NASDAQ's and NYSE's.
4. How do AIM's advocates defend it?
5. What do others say about AIM?

Translation

Please translate the part in waves into Chinese.

Questions for Discussion

1. What's your attitude towards AIM?
2. Do you think it is a good phenomenon that small firms are flooding AIM?

Unit 6

Passage

Shattered Faith
Li Weitao

Toshiba used to be a high flyer in China's notebook PC market, and had a firm hold on the top spot for four consecutive years prior to 2000. Yet its market share has since dropped to a level that the Japanese manufacturer would probably rather sweep under the proverbial carpet.

Many reasons have been proffered to explain Toshiba's fall from glory, including its complicated web of sales channels and networks throughout China. But one thing that cannot be ignored is a crisis of consumer trust that has contributed to the current lackluster performance, at least to a significant extent.

In 1999, Toshiba agreed to pay US $1.05 billion to about 500,000 US consumers to make up for a computer defect, an issue that was taken to court in the United States. But in China, the firm only posted a patch on its website and asked users to download it to fix the problem.

The backlash was huge. Many Chinese users accused Toshiba of discrimination. Chinese manufacturer Lenovo was quick to jump on this by offering better services. It has since grabbed the No. 1 market position.

To be fair, the media certainly didn't do Toshiba any favours. It's unlikely any company would have paid the same amount of money to Chinese consumers as it did in the United States. Business should be conducted under local laws and regulations, and Toshiba was not ordered by Chinese courts to compensate consumers. But this doesn't change the fact that the patch on its website was seen by many as simply inadequate.

Many Chinese consumers have a big, and sometimes blind, faith in foreign products. They tend to view these goods as guaranteeing superior quality and premium services.

Some foreign firms have let Chinese consumers down, however. Many big names are on this long list of disgraced multinationals, including Sony, SK Ⅱ, Nestlé and Mitsubishi Motors.

Food producers such as Kraft and Campbell are also on this list. Both companies were accused by Greenpeace of using genetically modified ingredients in their products sold in China. This violated the rights of Chinese consumers to clear access to information on the foods they buy.

This kind of corporate indifference could be ignored in the early days when multinationals were first starting to pour into the Chinese market. But local consumer awareness is much higher now. The times have changed, and Chinese shoppers now have higher expectations for quality and service.

This is why relatively expensive foreign products have become obvious targets for criticism. Unfortunately, a lot of multinationals have yet to come to terms with this harsh reality. Many foreign firms have been aggressively expanding their operations in China over the past several years, due to deregulation and wider access to the local market than in the past. Despite these developments, however, general levels of service have yet to improve accordingly.

I bought a flat-panel, Chinese brand TV last year, for example. It was roughly 40 percent cheaper than comparable foreign brands. I had some doubts about its quality after the TV was delivered to my home, so I called the company and a customer service representative showed up immediately. He patiently helped me adjust the TV's settings and readily offered me an opportunity to replace it with a new one. In the end, it turned out that the problem had nothing to do with quality.

A friend who bought a similar TV from a European brand was not so lucky, however. She called the company when problems arouse, but the manufacturer asked her to pay 500 yuan (US $62.5) so engineers could visit her home. These charges didn't include the cost of repairs or replacement parts. She was naturally furious, but this is common practice among foreign flat-panel manufacturers.

This stark contrast underlines how some foreign brands are losing ground in China.

Over the past several years, many Chinese firms have been aggressively improving their services, but some foreign companies have been slow to raise service levels in accordance with the expansion of their operations.

This is why some Chinese firms such as Haier and Lenovo are rapidly eating into their foreign counterparts' market share. Some have also attributed their rise to low-price strategies, however.

Some multinationals are even adopting "double standards" that seem to discriminate against Chinese consumers, especially in terms of after-sales services.

I assume that many overseas firms that have been slow to adapt to the rapidly changing Chinese market are still used to taking advantage of Chinese consumers' blind faith in foreign brands.

The problem is that consumers are not stupid. Eventually, these shoddy practices will catch up with foreign firms.

World Consumer Rights Day is on March 15, and Chinese media coverage of issues that violate consumer interests should be extensive. I am interested in reading how many foreign companies will be added to the increasingly long list of disgraced multinationals.

Words & Expressions

proverbial	adj.	widely known and spoken of
proffer	vt.	to present for acceptance or rejection
lackluster	adj.	lacking brilliance or vitality
backlash	n.	an adverse reaction to some political or social occurrence
jump on		to act quickly
premium	adj.	of higher than usual quality
deregulation	n.	the act of freeing from regulation (especially from governmental regulations)
stark	adj.	simple or obvious
shoddy	adj.	of inferior workmanship and materials; designed to deceive or mislead either deliberately or inadvertently
catch up with		to cause problems for sb.

Comprehension

1. What are the main reasons of the drop of Toshiba's market share in China?
2. How did Chinese manufacturer Lenovo grab the NO.1 market position in China?
3. What is the purpose of mentioning some multinationals, such as Sony, SK II, Nestlé and Mitsubishi Motors?
4. Why are some Chinese firms such as Haier and Lenovo rapidly eating into their foreign counterparts' market share?
5. Nowadays relatively expensive foreign products have become obvious targets for criticism. What are the reasons?

Translation

Please translate the parts in waves into Chinese.

Questions for Discussion

1. What do you think of the fact that some multinationals adopt "double standards" that seem to discriminate against Chinese consumers?
2. Talk about what you know about consumer rights.

Passage

China's Unwelcome Mat
Simon Elegant

Foreign firms are lining up to invest in China. But Beijing seems increasingly loath to let them in.

With his first official visit to China scheduled for this week, US Treasury Secretary Henry Paulson has been at pains to ease frictions between the world's two largest trading partners. Despite its ballooning trade deficit with China and the loss of American manufacturing jobs, the US remains a champion of open markets, Paulson said in a speech last Wednesday, noting: "Protectionist policies do not work and the collateral damage from these policies is high. We will not heed the siren songs of protectionism and isolationism."

China, meanwhile, was sending a very different message. The New China News Agency, known as Xinhua, released details last week of new regulations tightening control over distribution of information by foreign wire services. By forcing news agencies such as Reuters, Bloomberg and the Associated Press to distribute content through—and share revenue with—Xinhua, China was effectively rigging the market to favor its domestic news operation, critics charged—a claim bolstered by the publication of a speech in which Xinhua head Tian Congming said financial news was a "new growth engine" for the agency. Xinhua's power grab was also widely condemned overseas as an attempt to control the foreign media: among other restrictions, the rules prohibit dissemination of news that undermines "the fine cultural traditions of the Chinese nation". Oded Shenkar, a China expert at Ohio State University, says, "With a single move, they transfer a chunk of the highly profitable financial-news business from foreign to domestic hands and tighten control over the news. They manage to kill two birds with one stone."

Countering the critics, China's Premier Wen Jiabao insisted that Beijing "will ensure the freedom and the rights of the foreign news media and foreign financial information agencies". But alarm bells are nonetheless sounding in foreign boardrooms. In the past few months, Beijing has issued several regulations and is drafting more that appear to be aimed at limiting the ability of overseas firms to do business in China. Last week, China's stock-market regulator temporarily banned investment by foreign brokerages in domestic securities firms, citing the need to allow the local industry to consolidate so that Chinese firms would be large enough to compete with global giants. And in late August, the Ministry of Commerce issued new rules on mergers and acquisitions, including a number of vague provisions that appear to give the ministry wide powers to review and halt mergers. Bob Poole, who heads the Beijing office for the US-China Business Council, says there are good aspects to the changes—for example, they spell out previously unclear procedures for foreign purchases of Chinese companies. But he says some parts of the regulations are "not clear and might be used in a protectionist way".

Poole notes that similarly troubling provisions have been written into rules governing specific sectors in which foreign firms are active: heavy industries, express mail, banking and direct selling. With the five-year compliance period negotiated when China was admitted to the World Trade Organization due to end in a few months, he says it's critical that barriers lowered to gain WTO entry "should not be raised again in the form of technical regulation, industrial policies or other means".

Foreign access to China's huge market has become an incendiary issue on the mainland. Several recent acquisitions of large Chinese firms by foreign companies have been stalled after a storm of public protest over the impact such sales could have on China's economic security. A $375 million bid by the New York-based Carlyle Group for Xugong Group, China's leading construction-machinery manufacturer, has been delayed for 10 months. More recently, Chinese corporate officials and commentators condemned the proposed takeover of China's biggest manufacturer of kitchen goods, Supor Cookware, by the French firm SEB. One critic of such takeovers is the former head of China's National Statistics Administration, Li Deshui, who told a *China Daily* reporter, "If China lets multinationals' malicious mergers and acquisitions go ahead freely, China can act only as labor in the global supply chain."

Such complaints look set to intensify. Shenkar of Ohio State notes that almost two-thirds of China's exports are generated by companies with foreign investors, a figure that rises to nearly 80% in high-value-added sectors like IT. "There was far less foreign involvement in the economies of Korea or Japan at similar stages of growth," he says. "It's a serious weakness and has huge implications for national competitiveness and national security," Shenkar argues. China will have no choice but to use whatever methods it has to "recoup that lost share and build up a stable of companies that can be serious competitors on a global scale". Doing business in China has always been a challenge. For some, it may be about to become next to impossible.

Words & Expressions

friction	n.	conflict, as between persons having dissimilar ideas or interests; clash
collateral	adj.	coinciding in tendency or effect; concomitant or accompanying
protectionism	n.	the advocacy, system, or theory of protecting domestic producers by impeding or limiting, as by tariffs or quotas, the importation of foreign goods and services
isolationism	n.	a national policy of abstaining from political or economic relations with other countries
wire service		a news-gathering organization that distributes syndicated copy electronically to subscribers
rig	vt.	to manipulate dishonestly for personal gain
dissemination	n.	the act of dispersing or diffusing something
review	vt.	to look at again; examine again
halt	vt.	to stop from happening or developing
spell out		to make explicit; specify in detail
incendiary	adj.	arousing to action or rebellion
stall	vt.	to deliberately delay an event or action
malicious	adj.	intended to harm others
recoup	vt.	to regain or make up for

Comprehension

1. How do you understand the title of the text?
2. Why does the author say that China was effectively rigging the market to favor its domestic news operation?
3. How did China's Premier Wen Jiabao respond to criticism on regulations concerning distribution of information by foreign wire services?
4. What attitude does the author take toward doing business in China?
5. Is there any central idea in the text? If yes, then how does the author build the theme?

Translation

Please translate the part in waves into Chinese.

Questions for Discussion

1. What's the definition of protectionism? Do you agree with the statement that "trade protectionism: a double-edged sword"?
2. What are the proper policies China should adopt to develop its economy after its accession to WTO?

Unit 8

Passage

The Key Challenges Facing Corporate America at Present
Joel Shulman

Big companies don't seem to endure all that well. Despite all the advantages available to them (economies of scale, marketing savvy, strong channels of distribution), large corporations typically don't get bigger and stronger over time. Instead, they often become increasingly irrelevant and out of touch with the marketplace until eventually they are forced to close their doors. What's needed is a workable way to implant entrepreneurial thinking inside the corporate walls in such a way that wealth can be created on an ongoing basis.

Specifically, corporations face four key challenges:

1. Finding effective ways to renew the corporate spirit and stay vibrant and successful over an extended period of time;
2. Developing better ways to link employee compensation with the creation of long-term value;
3. Overcoming internal resistance to change;
4. Generating genuine growth in revenues and profits.

The Need for Corporate Renewal

Loads of ideas have already been tried to extend the life cycle of large corporations:
- In the 1960s, acquisitions were all the craze, with diversification as the main aim.
- In the 1970s, many companies tried to generate growth internally through intrapreneurship programs.
- During the 1980s, creating value through financial techniques (junk bonds, leveraged buyouts, financial asset repackaging) was tried.
- In the 1990s, corporate venture groups became the fashion, with spinoffs being taken to IPO stage as rapidly as possible.

All of these fads had their moment in the sun, but none have been able to extend the corporate life cycle appreciably. More than 80% of today's Fortune 500 companies have been in business for less than 100 years, and more than a third of the Fortune 500 companies are less than 25 years old. With very few exceptions, older companies don't keep gaining in strength over the years, but lose out to younger, more aggressive companies with new ideas.

Rampant Compensation Demands

At the present time, many organizations have executive compensation schemes which are poorly designed. Often, management is being rewarded for behavior which does not create long-term value for the shareholders. For example:

- Dealmakers—CEOs, investment bankers, venture capitalists and even high-profile consultants—typically make unprecedented amounts of money based solely on closing an acquisition, not on how the combined entity actually performs in the marketplace. This has created many corporate acquisitions which have lost significant shareholder value.
- Some CEOs have encouraged their organizations to take large short-term risks and then cashed out their options before the long-term problems appear.
- Many companies have used their own inflated stock to acquire other companies. Often, these acquisitions were made in the light of bidding wars which saw the acquiring company pay many billions more than the companies were worth, causing a number of flow-on problems.
- Some executives have traded away a better price for stockholders in an acquisition situation in exchange for more job security for themselves in the future.
- Many CEOs have more power and influence over their compensation level than they should. As a result, they are able to extract extraordinary levels of compensation for mediocre performance. During 1990–2000, CEO compensation increased by 1,300% while average employee salaries grew over the same period by 43%.

In all, the executive management teams of many organizations have titled their compensation systems to their own advantage. They devote more time to managing the company's stock price (so they can exercise their stock options) than they do to growing the business through organic growth or strategic expansion. There is a bias towards actions which will make an immediate impact on the company's stock price—mergers, divestitures, refinancing, equity carve-outs, venture funds, extensive layoffs and cost-cutting measures, strategic alliances and so forth.

Internal Resistance to Change

The long-term success of many firms has also been hampered by the resistance of middle management to change in the status quo. Or perhaps more accurately, many professional managers resist any proposed change which will reduce their own hard-won power and authority or future promotional opportunities.

Most businesses reward conformity more than innovation at the middle-manager level. There is a bias towards promoting those who toe the line which means the status quo becomes entrenched deeply in the business. Consequently, many middle-managers view themselves as the protectors of the corporate history, particularly in light of the fact CEOs come and go more rapidly these days. The middle-managers embody the culture of the company and will automatically resist any effort to change.

Corporate culture is another key issue. The culture sets the overall tone for an organization. It specifies which set of values, ethics and experiences will be deemed as desirable for the organization. The culture impacts on the organization's efficiency in a number of ways, formal and informal.

Due to the fact most of the work carried out by middle managers is hands-on, they can kill a new idea or a new project before it even gets a change to get off the ground. If the senior management of a company want to head off in some new direction, they need to spend the time and effort getting the middle managers on board first—otherwise, the new venture is to face some severe challenges.

Middle managers often focus on finding ways to spread their sphere of influence. Therefore, when a new growth initiative comes along, the criteria by which many middle managers will judge it is whether or not it will extend their sphere of influence. Or alternatively, a middle manager may view a new growth venture as a dumping ground to allocate costs so as to make their own department budgets look better. Either of these approaches can place a huge burden on a new business venture and point to the fact that often the best approach to generating new growth is to do so through independent business units rather than trying to overcome the resistance offered by middle managers.

Sluggish Corporate Growth

Every corporation aspires to grow, but not all growth is equal.

Specifically:

- There are times when two large companies merge to try and grow even more, but instead of growth only political infighting, redundant costs and expensive severance packages result.
- Some companies have used inappropriate techniques to boast explosive growth. This has worked well for a time, but ultimately results in loss of investor confidence and corporate failure.
- Managers, by and large, focus on revenue and asset growth. Shareholders are looking for increases in the stock price and shareholder returns. Sometimes, there is a marked difference between the two types of growth.
- At one time, managers expected to stay with one company for their entire careers. Nowadays, most managers anticipate they will be changing companies every three

to five years. That means there is less interest in initiating long-term projects which will require years of investment before sizable returns will be generated.

Because of these and other considerations, many managers have attempted to fast-track growth in recent times by pursing an acquisition strategy rather than attempting to generate organic or internal growth. Acquired growth, however, generates another set of problems:

- When companies merge, there are usually large layoffs to cull any duplicate job positions. This generates an intensive internal debate about who should go and who should stay, distracting attention from running the business.
- As employee morale deteriorates, internal distrust grows and collaboration goes out the window. So does the opportunity for teamwork on new growth initiatives.
- Attempting to combine the established culture of one business organization with that of another quite different entity is exceptionally difficult. The resulting conflicts are divisive and distracting.

As a result, acquired growth is never as good as growth that has been generated by market expansion, internal cost-cutting, intelligent choice of a strategic direction or the other old-fashioned ways of growing a company.

Words & Expressions

implant	vt.	to put firmly in the mind
buyout	n.	acquisition of a company by purchasing a controlling percentage of its stock
spinoff	n.	an unexpected but useful product or result of a process other than the main one
fad	n.	an interest followed with exaggerated zeal
rampant	adj.	unrestrained and violent
cash out		to exchange for cash
inflated	adj.	(of prices, costs, numbers, etc.) higher than they should be, or higher than people think is reasonable
mediocre	adj.	lacking exceptional quality or ability; moderate to inferior in quality
divestiture	n.	the sale by a company of a product line or a subsidiary or a division
toe the line		to do what is expected
infighting	n.	competition and disagreement, often bitter, which goes on between close members of a group, e.g. partners in a company or members of a political party

Comprehension
1. What are the key challenges facing corporate America at present?
2. Why do corporations need to renew themselves? And how to effectively manage the renewal process?
3. Why is there a bias towards actions which will make an immediate impact on the company's stock price?
4. What's the importance of corporate culture?
5. How do you understand the last paragraph of the article?

Translation
Please translate the parts in waves into Chinese.

Questions for Discussion
1. Talk about possible solutions to those key challenges.
2. Do you think Chinese corporations are facing the same challenges? And why?

Passage

The Management Process
Ricky W. Griffin & Ronald J. Ebert

Management is the process of planning, organizing, directing, and controlling an organization's financial, physical, human, and information resources to achieve its goals. Managers oversee the use of all these resources in their respective firms. All aspects of a manager's job are interrelated. In fact, any given manager is likely to be engaged in each of these activities during the course of any given day.

Planning

Determining what the organization needs to do and how to get it best done requires planning. Planning has three main components. As we have seen, it begins when managers determine the firm's goals. Next, they develop a comprehensive strategy for achieving those goals. After a strategy is developed, they design tactical and operational plans for implementing the strategy.

When Yahoo! < www. yahoo. com > was created, for example, the firm's top managers set a strategic goal of becoming a top firm in the then-emerging market for the Internet search engines. But then came the hard part—figuring out how to do it. They started by assessing the ways in which people actually use the Web and concluded that users wanted to be able to satisfy a wide array of needs, preferences, and priorities by going to as few sites as possible to find what they were looking for. Thus one key component of Yahoo!'s strategy was to foster partnerships and relationships with other companies so that potential Web surfers could draw upon several sources through a single portal—which would be Yahoo!. Thus, the goal of partnering emerged as one set of tactical plans for moving forward. Yahoo! managers then began fashioning alliances with such diverse partners as Reuters < www. reuters. com >, Standard & Poor's < www. standardpoor. com >, and the Associated Press < www. ap. org > (for news coverage), RE/Max < www. remax. com > (for real estate information), and a wide array of information providers specializing in sports, weather, entertainment, shopping, and travel. The creation of individual partnership agreements with each of these partners represents a form of operational planning.

Organizing

Once one of the leading-edge high-technology firms in the world, Hewlett-Packard <www. hewlett-packard. com> began to lose some of its luster in the mid-1990s. Ironically, one of the major reasons for its slide could be traced back to what had once been a major strength. Specifically, HP had long prided itself on being little more than a corporate confederation of individual businesses. Sometimes, these businesses even ended up competing among themselves. This approach had been beneficial for much of the firm's history: it was easier for each business to make its own decisions quickly and efficiently, and the competition kept each unit on its toes. By 1998, however, problems had become apparent, and no one could quite figure out what was going on.

Enter Ann Livermore, then head of the firm's software and services business. Livermore realized that the structure that had served so well in the past was now holding the firm back. To regain its competitive edge, HP needed an integrated, organization-wide Internet strategy. Unfortunately, the company's highly decentralized organization made that impossible. Livermore led the charge to create one organization to drive a single Internet plan. "I felt we could be the most powerful company in the industry," she says, "if we could get our hardware, software, and services aligned." In fact, a reorganized HP has bounced back and is quickly regaining its competitive strength.

This process—determining the best way to arrange a business's resources and activities into a coherent structure—is called organizing.

Directing

Managers have the power to give orders and demand results. Directing, however, involves more complex activities. When directing, a manager works to guide and motivate employees to meet the firm's objectives. Gordon Bethune, CEO of Continental Airline <www. continental. com>, is an excellent example of a manager who excels at motivating his employees. When he took the helm of the troubled carrier in 1994, morale was dismal, most employees hated their jobs, and the company's performance was among the worst in the industry.

Almost immediately, Bethune started listening to his employees to learn about their problems and hear how they thought the company could be improved. He also began to reward everyone when things went well and continued communicating with all Continental employees on a regular basis. Today, the firm is ranked among the best in the industry and is regularly identified as one of the best places to work in the United States. In May 2000, Continental was named the highest-quality airline in the United States, based on the J. D. Powers Survey of Customer Satisfaction.

Controlling

Controlling is the process of monitoring a firm's performance to make sure that the firm is meeting its goals. All CEOs must pay close attention to costs and performance. Indeed, skillful controlling, like innovative directing, is one reason that Gordon Bethune has been so successful at Continental. For example, the firm focuses almost relentlessly on numerous indicators of performance that can be constantly measured and adjusted. Everything from on-time arrivals to baggage-handling errors to the number of empty seats on an airplane to surveys of employee and customer satisfaction are regularly and routinely monitored. If on-time arrivals start to slip, Bethune focuses on the problem and gets it fixed. If a manager's subordinates provide less-than-glowing reviews, that manager loses part of his or her bonus. As a result, no single element of the firm's performance can slip too far before it's noticed and fixed.

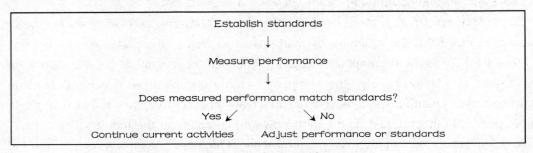

Figure 1 The Control Process

Figure 1 illustrates the control process that begins when management establishes standards, often for financial performance. If, for example, a company wants to increase sales by 20% over the next 10 years, then an appropriate standard might be an increase of about 2% a year.

Managers then measure actual performance against standards. If the two amounts agree, the organization continues along its present course. If they vary significantly, however, one or the other needs adjustment. If sales have increased 2.1% by the end of the first year, things are probably fine. If sales have dropped 1%, some revision in plans may be needed. Perhaps the original goal should be lowered or more money should be spent on advertising. Control can also show where performance is running better than expected and thus serve as a basis for providing rewards or reducing costs. For example, when Ford recently introduced the new Explorer Sports Trac (an SUV with a pickup bed), initial sales were so strong the firm was able to delay a major advertising campaign for three months because it was selling all of the vehicles it could make anyway.

Words & Expressions

management	n.	process of planning, organizing, directing, and controlling an organization's resources to achieve its goals
planning	n.	management process of determining what an organization needs to do and how to get it best done
component	n.	any of the parts that together make a whole system
assess	vt.	to place a value on; judge the worth of something
draw upon		to make use of
fashion	vt.	to make out of components (often in an improvising manner)
luster	n.	a quality that outshines the usual
confederation	n.	a union of political or economic organizations
keep on one's toes		to keep in the state of being alert
hold ... back		to keep something from developing
organizing	n.	management process of determining how to best arrange an organization's resources and activities into a coherent structure
directing	n.	management process of guiding and motivating employees to meet an organization's objectives
take the helm of		to hold in control of; be in charge of
controlling	n.	management process of monitoring an organization's performance to ensure that it is meeting its goals
monitoring	n.	keeping tabs on; keeping an eye on; keeping under surveillance

Comprehension

1. What does the management process include?
2. What are the main components of planning? Based on the Yahoo!'s example in the article, please explain how they work.
3. What's the major reason for the slide of Hewlett-Packard? What do you think is the effective way to save it?
4. How can others benefit from the example of Gordon Bethune?
5. What does Figure 1 "The Control Process" try to illustrate? Do you agree with it? And why?

Translation

Please translate the part in waves into Chinese.

Questions for Discussion
1. Say what you know about management.
2. Describe the four activities that constitute the management process, and explain how they relate to each other.

Unit 10

Passage

China Must Slow Down a Bit

A China-Centric Asia

By looking at Asia through the PPP-based lens, there can be little doubt as to the region's newfound China dominance. The IMF puts China's share in the world economy at 12.7%, well in excess of Japan's 7.1% share and India's 4.8% portion, the next two largest economies in the region. But there's more to Asia's China centricity than its role as the region's increasingly dominant producer. China's voracious appetite for imports—up an astonishing 40% alone in 2003—underscores the increasingly powerful trade linkages that China exerts on the rest of the world. Its Asian trading partners are the biggest beneficiaries of China's external impetus. For example, over the 12 months of 2003, surging exports to China accounted for 32% of Japan's total increase in exports; for Korea, the number was 36%, whereas in China's Taiwan, fully 68% of the last year's export growth can be accounted for by surging shipments to Mainland of China.

The combination of urbanization, demand for new infrastructure, and the rapid expansion of its manufacturing platform, has had a profound impact on China's consumption of industrial materials and its related impact on global commodity markets. Whereas this nation had a share of only about 4% of global nominal GDP in 2003, it accounted for 7% of the world's total consumption of the crude oil, 31% of global coal, 30% of iron ore, 27% of steel products, 25% of aluminum, and fully 40% of the world's cement consumption. There can be no mistaking China's ascendancy as the new engine of the Asian economy.

China Slowdown

Yet China must now slow down, and so all of the above are at risk. From Premier Wen Jiabao on down, senior officials in China have been unanimous in sending a clear signal that they are utterly determined to engineer a slowdown. Yet the incoming data flow on the Chinese economy shows what they are up against: GDP growth held at 9.7% in the first quarter of 2004, boosted by an outsize 43% surge in fixed investment spending. Moreover, bank lending rebounded sharply in the early months of 2004 after having decelerated in the final quarter of 2003. The overheating of the Chinese economy is very much a by-product of the interplay between excessive bank lending and runaway investment spending. These are the main sources of the problem that the Chinese leadership is now prepared to attack head-on.

That attack is now under way. China's campaign of policy restraint was initiated last fall, with an increase in reserve requirements on bank deposits from 6% to 7% announced in late August and made effective in late September. That measure apparently didn't work in arresting the rapid growth of the real economy. And so Premier Wen has been quite direct in warning that further forceful measures were being prepared to stem the excesses of bank lending. True to his word, the People's Bank of China unveiled a second tightening in late March and then a third action in early April. A failure to arrest the excesses of an overheated economy is perceived to be a recipe for the dreaded hard landing. China cannot afford such a dire outcome. It would have serious implications for unemployment and nonperforming bank loans, thereby undermining the very reforms that are at the heart of the China miracle. The verdict is clear: the Chinese leadership now senses a new urgency in bringing its economy under control. The latest monetary tightening measures should be viewed as warning signs of more such initiatives to come.

Adjustment

China has emerged as the unquestioned engine of pan-regional growth, but now the Chinese economy is in need of a major adjustment of its own. The Chinese consumer does not qualify as a new Asian powerhouse. As my colleague Andy Xie has noted, the consumption share of Chinese GDP fell to a record low of 54% in 2003 down markedly from the 59% average of the 1990s and the 65% average of the 1980s. Sure, there are some signs of sharply improving consumption trends in China's coastal region, but the comparisons are against a very low base. For example, domestic car sales surged 70% last year to 1.7 million units; however, with an urban population now in excess of 520 million, new vehicle penetration remains remarkably low.

The macro case for Chinese consumption demand remains difficult. With job losses from ongoing reforms of state-owned enterprises still estimated at 7-9 million annually, and with China's workforce lacking the safety net of social security, private sector pensions and retraining programs, the Chinese consumer remains predisposed toward saving. That shows up very clearly in the numbers: household saving deposits rose to 89% of Chinese GDP by the end of 2003, up from 62% in 1997. Autonomous support from private consumption in China remains at least 3-5 years away.

Words & Expressions

in excess of		more than
voracious	adj.	very eager for something, especially a lot of food
underscore	vt.	to emphasize or show that sth. is important or true
ascendancy	n.	the position of having power or influence over sb./sth.
engineer	vt.	to arrange for sth. to happen or take place
outsize	adj.	larger than the usual size
decelerate	vi.	to become or make sth. become slower
arrest	vt.	to stop a process or a development; prevent, curb, restrain
bring ... under control		to be dealt with or limited successfully
ongoing	adj.	continuing to exist or develop

Comprehension

1. What is China's position in Asia?
2. What caused the overheating of the Chinese economy? And what showed the overheating of the Chinese economy?
3. What measures have the Chinese government taken?
4. Why does Chinese consumption demand remain difficult?
5. How do you look at China's economic development?

Translation

Please translate the part in waves into Chinese.

Questions for Discussion

1. what do you think of China's current property market?
2. what do you think of China's economic development?

Unit 11

Passage

Changes and Challenges
Robert Lawrence Kuhn

China makes news. Stories about corporate takeovers, trade disputes, diplomatic rivalries and military tensions fill the American media, and scare screeds about "Communist China" that sound like Cold War satire are taken seriously.

Consistent bilateral relations between America and China are essential for the peace and prosperity of the 21st century, and for this reason such misperceptions are disturbing and potentially dangerous. Americans should know the inner attitudes and primary concerns of China's new leaders, especially those of President Hu Jintao.

Recent history provides backdrop.

After a century of foreign subjugation and decades of ideologically induced oppression, Deng Xiaoping initiated revolutionary reforms in 1978, two years after Mao Zedong's death. These reforms became irreversible and the economy developed dramatically during the period of Jiang Zemin's leadership from 1989 to 2002.

When asked what I've seen to be the country's greatest change since I first came to China in 1989, I answer that economic development, as remarkable and historic as it has been, is China's second most important change. China's greatest change is the mentality and spirit of its people—their attitudes and outlooks, expansive thinking, confidence in themselves and their country, and enthusiasm to reach out to the world.

But China has serious, systemic problems—income disparity, fragile financial systems, sustainable development, unemployment, migrant workers, corruption, energy constraints, environmental pollution, family and moral values, and more. Some problems result from dramatic economic growth; some from rapid transition to a market economy; some from need of social and political reform.

President Hu acknowledged that "the problems and contradictions China will face in the next decades may be even more complicated and thorny than others ... with its social structure and ideological set-up also in major shake-up." Furthermore independent thinking of the general public, their newly developed penchant for independent choices and thus the widening gap of ideas among different social strata will pose further challenges to China's policy makers.

China's fundamental problem is a dependency on growth combined with a widening gap between the rich and the poor, imbalances that the Communist Party calls China's "most serious social problem". China must grow because, with tens of millions of farmers needing to be relocated to cities, millions of workers laid off from state-owned enterprises, and with legions of young people entering the workforce, unemployment could threaten social stability.

President Hu Jintao is now faced with the natural consequences of the country's prodigious economic transformation, which has spawned complex and interwoven challenges. China's leaders know that they must be flexible, innovate, consider diverse opinions, and make measured decisions.

President Hu's overarching vision is summarized by three slogans—"Harmonious Society" (*he xie she hui*) and "Scientific Development Perspective" (*ke xue fa zhan guan*) domestically, and "Peaceful Rise" (*he ping jue qi*) internationally. Harmonious Society stresses social and political reform and seeks fairness and equity across China's diverse populations and geographies; Scientific Development Perspective stresses integrated sets of solutions to arrays of economic, social and environmental problems, and seeks the rectification of economic imbalances and the institutionalization of sustainable development; and Peaceful Rise conveys that no matter how strong China will become, it will remain a bulwark of stability in the world and it will never threaten its neighbours.

One application of Scientific Development Perspective is the recent rejection by a coastal county of a large investment in a battery factory because of pollution. Another is a huge investment by the municipality of Tianjin in a world-class hospital (Tianjin Medical University General Hospital) with a "Health Management Centre" to promote healthy lifestyles and prevent illness.

It is true that many of China's current problems are the inevitable side effects of rapid economic development, which, of necessity, had to occur in an unbalanced way. Without economic development, everyone is equal but poor—everyone is equally poor. China must prevent the trauma of social disruptions by getting out ahead of the historical trends and implementing sophisticated, nuanced policies. Economic development had to come first, but now a more complex agenda of social and political requirements must be integrated and optimized with pure economic growth. This is the only way to represent the fundamental interests of the people and this is the primary thrust of President Hu's Scientific Development Perspective.

Hu Jintao continues the Party's modernization, calling for both "advancement" of the Party and its increasing transparency, thus creating a "democracy of the elite" (which is my term, not China's), which means increasing democracy within the Party and the Party continuing to lead the country. President Hu's political philosophy stresses closeness to people; people first; transparency in government; increasing democracy and openness in the Party; progressive democracy in society (where propitious); continued economic development; and an all-around pragmatism. Hu's commitment to promote democracy is tempered by the higher good of social stability.

Western criticism of President Hu, particularly regarding human rights, highlights his sensitivity to social stability but misses his fresh commitment to address China's multifaceted problems. Hu's pragmatic, non-ideological agenda has three core values—maintaining social stability to further economic development; instituting social fairness and rectifying imbalances; and sustaining Chinese culture to secure national sovereignty and enrich people's lives. Such realism increases confidence that China, notwithstanding its problems, will maintain its remarkable development.

What emerges in President Hu's view is the "China Model", a systematic approach to national structure and development that combines dynamic economic growth, a free market energized by a vigorous "non-public" (private) sector, concern for the welfare of all citizens, cultural enrichment, and a synergistic approach to rectify economic imbalances (Scientific Development Perspective) and ensure social fairness—all of which lead, in Hu's vision, to a Harmonious Society. Beijing sees its China Model as an alternative to Washington's Western Democracy Model, particularly for developing countries.

In President Hu's words, "A harmonious society should feature democracy, the rule of law, equality, justice, sincerity, amity and vitality." Such a society, he says, will give full scope to people's talent and creativity, enable all the people to share the wealth brought by reform and development, and forge an ever closer bond between the people and government.

Words & Expressions

screed	n.	a long piece of writing
misperception	n.	(a) wrong or incorrect perception
backdrop	n.	the situation or place in which something happens
subjugation	n.	gaining control of (a country, etc.); subduing; conquering
disparity	n.	difference or inequity
shake-up	n.	major reform or reorganization
penchant	n.	(from French) a special liking for something
strata	n.	(pl. of stratum) level of class in society
legion	n.	large number of people
prodigious	adj.	very great in size, amount or degree, so as to cause amazement or admiration; enormous

spawn	vt.	to produce, generate, result in, give rise to, usu. in great numbers
overarching	adj.	affecting or including everything, and therefore very important
bulwark	n.	person or thing that supports, defends or protects
trauma	n.	a physical wound or a psychic injury
nuanced	adj.	having or characterized by nuances
thrust	n.	main point or theme
propitious	adj.	giving or indicating a good chance of success, favorable
temper	vt.	to moderate or soften the effects of sth.; mitigate sth.
notwithstanding	prep.	without being affected by (sth.); in spite of
synergistic	adj.	working together; used especially of groups, as subsidiaries of a corporation, cooperating for an enhanced effect
amity	n.	friendly relationship between people or countries

Comprehension

1. What changes have taken place in China according to the author?
2. How can China resolve the problems mentioned in this passage?
3. What are the three slogans and what do they mean?
4. What are the side effects of rapid economic development? What's your own attitude towards this phenomenon?
5. Can you give an account of "China Model"?

Translation

Please translate the parts in waves into Chinese.

Questions for Discussion

1. What do you think are China's main current changes and challenges?
2. Discuss the conflicts between industrial development and environmental pollution. Which do you prefer, a well-developed country with poor environment and a poor country with agreeable environment?

Unit 12

Passage

Can Asia-Pacific Go the EU Way?

The EU experience highlights several issues which are important for Asia-Pacific integration.

First, European integration emerged from a specific political and economic context. It was created with a twofold purpose: to reconstruct the economy after the second World War and to promote peace and prosperity on the continent on the basis of shared democratic and liberal economic values. The existence of this common objective strongly supported by the political commitment and leadership of France and Germany was crucial to successful unification. Post-war economic conditions were also favourable for European integration, marked by rapid economic growth, strong commercial ties and the relative homogeneity of the founding members of the European Community, most of them small and medium-sized open economies.

The absence of a shared political objective and a clear vision for long-term cooperation will make Asia-Pacific integration more difficult to achieve. In marked contrast to Europe, regionalism in Asia-Pacific has so far been driven by market considerations, in other words by external considerations. European integration was the result of a strategic choice shaped by internal dynamics.

This does not mean that Asian regionalism should await greater convergence of national economies. Initial conditions, although important, are not decisive factors in economic integration. In the early years of European integration, some countries had lower per capita incomes than others, but they all joined the EU.

Europe's example suggests that Asia-Pacific's more developed countries should take the lead and push for a process of economic integration based on a common denominator. Regional development cooperation initiatives could be taken by a core group of leading countries which would act as facilitators of growth and convergence of national economies by pooling resources and establishing common projects to help less developed and poorer countries to absorb the shocks of trade liberalization. The European Structural Funds provide a good illustration of an initiative that supports the principles of regional solidarity and convergence of national economies.

Second, Europe's successful economic and monetary integration has been achieved because of gradual and pragmatic sequencing that involved modest initial steps within a long-term vision. The process started modestly with trade integration and fixed-but-adjustable exchange rates. Once the common market was fully developed and exchange rates stabilized (a process that took nearly 30 years), capital markets were liberalized and macroeconomic cooperation enshrined in the Economic and Monetary Union. European integration has therefore proceeded in evolutionary steps.

Monetary and financial cooperation in Asia-Pacific regionalism, however, is more a reaction to new economic and financial risks emerging from globalization. It did not emerge through an evolutionary process. However, as trade cooperation is advancing rapidly, the need for better currency management system and deeper monetary and financial integration is fast becoming necessary at least for selected East and South-East Asian countries.

Third, one crucial aspect of European integration is that it has created supranational institutions and relied on the political willingness to surrender national sovereignty in a number of policies to these institutions. In the event of conflicts of national interests, long-term cooperation efforts inevitably fail without the presence of a third party. Europe has developed multinational entities in charge of defending economic integration (European Commission, European Central Bank), mechanisms for compensating the losers (Structural Funds, CAP) and a common jurisdiction to solve conflicts between national laws and common rules.

In Asia-Pacific, by contrast, there are subregional efforts to develop supranational institutions but there is very little region-wide institutionalization. Furthermore, while EU regulations are mostly binding and supported by a system of sanctions, the Asia-Pacific regional frameworks issue non-binding "declarations" and "plans of actions". Supranational institutions, which are a key force for integration in Europe, do not exist in the Asia-Pacific region.

Moreover, in Europe, from the outset there has been a good internal balance between the leading economies. Notwithstanding the relatively high level of trust that existed among the founding members of the EU and the crucial importance of political will as a driving factor of institution-building, an important element worth highlighting is that the loss of national sovereignty in key areas was accompanied by strong compensation mechanisms.

In Asia-Pacific, already established economic powers (Japan and Korea) and a rapidly emerging one (China) dominate the economic scene, and India is taking on a more significant role. These large players can play a crucial part in developing an "Asian way of integration".

Words & Expressions

homogeneity	n.	the quality of being similar or comparable in kind or nature
European Community		an international organization of European countries formed after World War II to reduce trade barriers and increase cooperation among its members
dynamic	n.	force that produces change, action, or effects
convergence	n.	the occurrence of two or more things coming together
denominator	n.	an average level or standard
facilitator	n.	a person who makes the process of an activity easier
pool	vt.	to put (money, resources, etc) into a common fund
enshrine	vt.	to place or keep sth. (in, or as if in, a shrine or holy place)
binding	adj.	imposing or commanding adherence to a commitment, an obligation, or a duty
sanction	n.	the penalty for noncompliance specified in a law or decree

Comprehension

1. Why is it more difficult to achieve Asia-Pacific integration compared with European integration?
2. What kind of role should Asia-Pacific's more developed countries play in the realization of integration of this area?
3. Why does the author say European integration is an evolutionary process? How about the Asia-Pacific integration?
4. What is a supranational institution? How do such institutions function in the European integration?
5. What can the Asia-Pacific learn from the European integration?

Translation
Please translate the part in waves into Chinese.

Questions for Discussion

1. What kinds of obstacles do you think the Asia-Pacific will come across in its integration?
2. What's the prospect of Asian-Pacific integration?

Passage

Economic Growth Promotes Regional Financial Cooperation in Asia

Economic Outlook for ASEAN +3

Last year saw significant economic fluctuations for most ASEAN+3 countries. In the first half of 2003, the weakening global economy, uncertainties surrounding the war in Iraq, and the outbreak of SARS contributed to a slowdown in GDP growth for many of these economies. Although signs of improvements were visible in early August last year, our assessment of the economic situation was one of cautious optimism. However, since then, the economic situation has taken a turn for the better. The ASEAN+3 countries, taken together, posted GDP growth of 4% in 2003—considerably better than the 2.4% growth foreseen earlier. Among the countries that performed better than expected were Thailand, Japan, PRC, and Malaysia. A number of developments in recent months suggest that the economic outlook for ASEAN+3 will continue to be very positive.

First, the external economic environment facing ASEAN+3 has vastly improved in recent months. There is increasing evidence that the US economic recovery is strengthening. There were concerns about the pace of job creation, but there are signs of improvement. US GDP is now forecast to grow by 4.6% this year. The current forecast of the Euro area's GDP growth for this year, at close to 2%, is much higher than last year.

Second, Japan's economy is continuing to exceed expectations. Fourth quarter annualized GDP growth last year was a better-than-expected 6.4%, and GDP growth for 2003 reached 2.7%, much higher than the 0.9% forecast made in August 2003. GDP is now forecast to grow by 3% this year.

Third, the recent buoyancy in intra-regional trade among ASEAN+3 countries is another factor that argues well for the region's growth prospects. Intra-regional trade among ASEAN+3 now accounts for about 35% of the region's total exports, partly driven by the strong growth in the People's Republic of China.

Finally, within ASEAN+3, domestic demand remains strong in several countries, and this should continue to support growth. In Japan, while growth was driven primarily by exports in the initial phase of the current recovery, domestic demand is increasingly becoming a significant source of growth. Among other countries, domestic demand, especially fixed investment, is growing at an exceptionally high pace in the PRC, while in the last two years consumer spending accounted for about one third of the GDP growth in Indonesia and Malaysia. There are also tentative signs that private investment, after remaining subdued for some time, is starting to pick up in some of the crisis-affected countries, especially in Thailand.

Taking into account these positive developments at the regional and non-regional levels, the ASEAN+3 countries as a whole are forecast to grow by 4.3% this year. This is almost two percentage points higher than the forecast of 2.4%. Besides, given the emerging positive economic trends in Japan, an upward revision to next year's growth forecast cannot be ruled out.

These forecasts are subject to risks, including the political uncertainties associated with this year's elections in several of these countries, worldwide geopolitical tensions and terrorism, and the large global current account imbalances.

There are also concerns that the recent increase in international commodity prices could ignite inflationary pressures. Yet, given the current low inflation environment and excess production capacities in several sectors in the region, it is unlikely to cause a major turnaround in inflation and harm the current growth trend.

The region should, however, be prepared to adjust to a possible increase in US interest rates. For those ASEAN+3 countries that follow a flexible exchange rate policy, a US rate hike need not necessarily mean higher domestic interest rates. Even for those regional economies that have fixed exchange rates with the US dollars, domestic interest rates could be kept low, as many of these countries also hold sizable foreign exchange reserves. A possible US interest rate hike need not necessarily undermine continued strong growth among the ASEAN+3 countries.

Regional Monetary and Financial Cooperation

Before the 1997 financial crisis, regional cooperation among the ASEAN+3 countries largely focused on trade and investment. Since the crisis, this work has continued, but a new dimension—monetary and financial cooperation—has been added. ASEAN + 3's regional monetary and financial cooperation initiatives fall into three broad categories: information exchange and policy dialogue, reserve sharing and pooling, and regional bond market development. And in the sphere of bond market development, for the first time, concrete steps are being taken at the regional level under the Asian Bond Market Initiative.

ASEAN+3 is now approaching a critical point with these initiatives. First, the 1997 crisis may be over; yet, in an increasingly integrated global economy, a new crisis may strike without much warning. The key issue is how the next steps under these regional initiatives should be sequenced, and at what speed they should proceed.

One option is to institutionalize the process by establishing an independent, technical body—a regional policy dialogue unit—and a higher-level decision-making body, a regional surveillance group, over the next two years or so. The regional policy dialogue unit should function as an information resource on the state of the regional economics, and as an independent analyst of regional economic developments and policy issues. It should submit regular reports on macroeconomic and financial market conditions in participating countries to a regional surveillance group.

The CMI has proven a commendable initiative in the aftermath of the 1997 crisis. But this is relatively small compared to both the foreign exchange reserves held by member countries and the emergency assistance provided to these countries during the 1997 financial crisis. There is, therefore, merit in expanding the size of CMI swaps, or consider earmarking a portion of the foreign exchange reserves for financing short-term liquidity needs of the member countries. Subsequently, say, over the three- to five-year horizon, the region could also consider establishing a centralized reserve pool.

Bond market development has long been an important issue for ADB's developing member countries. For the first time, concrete steps are being taken at the regional level. These initiatives should be vigorously pursued over the next several years.

Words & Expressions

fluctuation	n.	the quality of being unsteady and subject to changes
buoyancy	n.	the tendency to rise
subdue	vt.	to put down by force or intimidation or authority
revision	n.	the act of revising or altering (involving reconsideration and modification)
inflation	n.	a general rise in the prices of services and goods in a particular country, resulting in a fall in the value of money
inflationary	adj.	causing or connected with a general rise in the prices of services and goods
turnaround	n.	a situation in which sth. changes from bad to good
hike	n.	a large or sudden increase in prices, cost
sequence	vt.	to arrange in a sequence or order
surveillance	n.	close observation of a person or group (usually by the police)
aftermath	n.	the consequences of an event (especially a catastrophic event)
earmark	vt.	to give or assign a resource to a particular person or cause

Comprehension

1. What causes significant economic fluctuations for most ASEAN+3 countries?
2. Why is US economy so important? And why does its economic recovery have

something to do with the global economy?
3. Why does the author say the economic outlook for ASEAN+3 will continue to be very positive?
4. What do ASEAN+3's regional monetary and financial cooperation initiatives include?
5. What are the functions of the regional policy dialogue unit?

Translation
Please translate the parts in waves into Chinese.

Questions for Discussion
1. Say what you know about ASEAN.
2. Talk about possible ways to raise money for a company.

How Higher Oil Prices Affect the Global Economy

Oil prices remain an important determinant of global economic performance.

Overall, an oil-price increase leads to a transfer of income from importing to exporting countries through a shift in the terms of trade. The magnitude of the direct effect of a given price increase depends on the share of the cost of oil in national income, the degree of dependence on imported oil and the ability of end-users to reduce their consumption and switch away from oil. It also depends on the extent to which gas prices rise in response to an oil-price increase, the gas-intensity of the economy and the impact of higher prices on other forms of energy.

How Higher Oil Prices Affect the Global Economy

Naturally, the bigger the oil-price increase and the longer higher prices are sustained, the bigger the macroeconomic impact. For net oil-exporting countries, a price increase directly increases real national income through higher export earnings, though part of this gain would be later offset by losses from lower demand for exports generally due to the economic recession suffered by trading partners.

Higher oil prices lead to inflation, increased input costs, reduced non-oil demand and lower investment in net oil-importing countries. Tax revenues fall and the budget deficit increases, which drives interest rates up.

An oil price increase typically leads to upward pressure on nominal wage levels. Wage pressures together with reduced demand tend to lead to higher unemployment, at least in the short term. The more sudden and the more pronounced the prices increase, the greater these effects are, and the effects are magnified by the impact of higher prices on consumer and business confidence.

An oil-price increase also changes the balance of trade between countries and exchange rates. Net oil-importing countries normally experience a deterioration in their balance of payments, putting downward pressure on exchange rates. As a result, imports become more expensive and exports less valuable, leading to a drop in real national income. Without a change in central bank and government monetary policies, the dollar may tend to rise as oil-producing countries' demand for dollar-denominated international reserve assets grow.

The economic and energy-policy response to a combination of higher inflation, higher unemployment, lower exchange rates and lower real output also affects the overall impact on the economy over the longer term. Government policy cannot eliminate the adverse impacts described above but it can minimize them. Similarly, inappropriate policies can worsen them.

Overly contractionary monetary and fiscal policies to contain inflationary pressures could exacerbate the recessionary income and unemployment effects. On the other hand, expansionary monetary and fiscal policies may simply delay the fall in real income necessitated by the increase in oil prices, stoke up inflationary pressures and worsen the impact of higher prices in the long run.

While the general mechanism by which oil prices affect economic performance is generally understood, the precise dynamics and magnitude of these effects are uncertain.

Quantitative estimates of the overall macroeconomic damage caused by past oil price shocks and the gains from the 1986 price collapse to the economics of oil-importing countries vary substantially. This is partly due to differences in the models used to examine the issue.

Nonetheless, the effects were certainly significant: economic growth fell sharply in most oil-importing countries in the two years following the price hikes of 1973 – 1974 and 1979 – 1980. Indeed, most of the major economic downturns in the United States, Europe and the Pacific since the 1970s have been preceded by sudden increases in the price of crude oil, although other factors were more important in some cases.

Similarly, the boost to economic growth in oil-exporting countries provided by higher oil prices in the past has always been less than the loss of economic growth in importing countries, such that the net effect has always been negative. The growth of the world economy has always fallen sharply in the wake of each major run-up in oil prices, including that of 1999 – 2000.

The results of the sustained higher oil price simulation for both the OECD and non-OECD countries suggest that, as has always been the case in the past, the net effect on the global economy would be negative. That is, the economic stimulus provided by higher oil (and gas) export earnings in OPEC and other exporting countries would be outweighed by the depressive effect of higher prices on economic activity in the importing countries, at least in the first year or two following the price rise.

Combining the results of all world regions yields a net fall of around 0.5% in global GDP—equivalent to \$255 billion—in the first year of higher prices. The loss of GDP would diminish somewhat by 2008 as increased demand from oil-exporting countries boosts the exports and GDP of oil-importing countries. The transfer of income from oil importers to oil exporters in the year following the $10 price increase would amount to roughly $150 billion.

Impact on Financial Markets

Higher oil prices, by affecting economic activity, corporate earnings and inflation, would also have major implications for financial markets notably equity values, exchange rates and government financing.

International capital market valuations of equity debt in oil-importing countries would be revised downwards and those in oil-exporting countries upwards.

Fiscal imbalances in oil-importing countries caused by lower income would be exacerbated in those developing countries, like India and Indonesia that continue to provide direct subsidies on oil products to protect poor households and domestic industry. The burden of subsidies tends to grow as international prices rise, adding to the pressure on government budgets and increasing political and social tensions.

The loss of business and consumer confidence resulting from an oil shock could lead to significant shifts in levels and patterns of investment, savings and spending. A loss of confidence and inappropriate policy responses, especially in the oil-importing countries, could amplify the economic effects in the medium term.

Words & Expressions

offset	vt.	to balance one influence against an opposing influence, so that there is no great difference as a result
recession	n.	a difficult time for the economy of a country, when there is less trade and industrial activity than usual and more people are unemployed
drive... up		to make sth. (such as prices) rise quickly
magnify	vt.	to make sth. bigger, louder or stronger
deterioration	n.	process of changing to an inferior state
adverse	adj.	negative and unpleasant; not likely to produce a good result
contractionary	adj.	of contracting or of being contracted
exacerbate	vt.	to make sth. worse, especially a disease or problem
expansionary	adj.	encouraging economic expansion
stoke up		*to make people feel sth. more strongly*
dynamics	n.	the way in which people or things behave or react to each other in a particular situation
downturn	n.	a time when the economy becomes weaker
outweigh	vt.	to be greater or more important than sth.

subsidy　　　　　　n.　　money that is paid by a government or an organization to reduce the costs of services or of producing goods so that their prices can be kept low

Comprehension
1. How do higher oil prices affect oil-importing countries?
2. How do higher oil prices affect oil-exporting countries?
3. What can government do to protect the economy?
4. What is the net effect of higher oil prices on the global economy?
5. Summarize the way in which higher oil prices affect the financial market.

Translation
Please translate the parts in waves into Chinese.

Questions for Discussion
1. What caused changes of oil prices?
2. How can one country protect its economy from the changing oil prices?

Waste Not Want Not

Lance Maughan

How could China lead the over-consuming West towards sustainable economic development?

China can decide if the world moves towards sustainable economic development, according to a new report warning that rapidly growing Asian economies are using natural resources at a faster rate than previously reported. The WWF Asia Pacific 2005 Ecological Footprint and Ecological Wealth Report, published recently in Chinese, shows that people in the region are devouring resources at nearly double the rate it can support. "China is in a unique position to shape the world's path to sustainable development in the coming decades," said Dermot O'Gorman, Country Representative, WWF China. "If China, where around 20 percent of the world's population lives, can get the balance right between natural resource consumption and production, we could see a very different future than the current projections."

Rapidly growing populations and massive economic development have led to a trebling in consumption of natural resources in the Asia-Pacific Region over the past 40 years. The Asia-Pacific Region could consume less, pollute less and tread more lightly on the planet without harming economic growth and competitiveness, suggests the report, which explores the impact of humans in 149 of the world's major countries on populations of wild species as well as land and water. As a processing hub and an important link in the supply chain for many developed countries, "China has the potential to help reduce the impact of consumers in the EU and US, which consume an unequal share of global resources."

More resource-efficient buildings and transport networks in major cities are crucial if China is to build a sustainable economy, report authors suggest. Encouraging innovation in new energy technologies that would free China from the high cost of fossil fuel imports is also recommended, as is "investing in solutions for promoting sustainability in the areas of food, health, nature management, transportation, and shelter." Report authors recommend withdrawing investments from "industries that are obstacles to sustainability".

But China may find it hard to be discerning. Foreign investment has been crucial to the export boom that has turned China into the world's third-largest trading nation. The country attracted more than US $60 billion in foreign direct investment in 2005 from foreign firms keen to take advantage of the country's low wages and huge domestic market. Foreign-owned firms account for almost 60 percent of the country's exports, but most of those exports so far come from the kind of high labor, high polluting manufacturing. Caught in a dilemma, China will have to choose between cleaner industries and the jobs they bring.

A solution may be to hand. A long-awaited plan to unify the tax rate paid by domestic and foreign-invested companies could weed mucky manufacturing FDI out, believes Xing Houyuan, a senior researcher at the Chinese Academy of International Trade and Economic Cooperation, a think tank under the Ministry of Commerce. "I expect foreign investment in sectors such as manufacturing, processing and real estate will shrink, but investment might increase in the services sector when it opens wider to the outside in 2006," said Xing. No date has been set for a unified business tax rate but preferential income tax rates as low as 15 percent set by local authorities (domestic firms are typically taxed at 33 percent) have helped China rake in more than US $1 billion a week in mostly manufacturing FDI since it joined the World Trade Organization in late 2001.

China has already been signaling it wants cleaner investment. Foreign exhibitors at the recent Texcare Asia Expo in Beijing were quizzed by buyers about water and energy efficient machinery, said Engelbert Heinz, managing director of Kannegiesser, a German-based manufacturer of laundry machines. "Solutions to save water and energy are very topical in China at the moment," said Heinz. "Suppliers," he added, "are scrambling to build special efficient machines for China to take part of a market driven by a growing middle class, increasing awareness about hygiene and a rash of new hotels and hospitals being built."

"China-bound foreign investment will shift toward services and away from manufacturing," said Tang Min, chief economist at the Asian Development Bank in Beijing. "Some of the labor-intensive, cheap labor type of export-orientated FDI will gradually move more to the center of China and, if not, move out of the country," he said. New policies that attract investment into the interior may help China assume the role urged on it by the WWF Asia Pacific 2005 Ecological Footprint and Ecological Wealth Report.

The Asia-Pacific Region now contributes to 40 percent of the world's use of resources such as food, fiber, energy and water. According to the report, their ecological footprint—their resource demand on earth—is 1.7 times higher than the rate at which Asia-Pacific's ecosystems can regenerate. China has doubled its ecological footprint during the 40 years from 1961 to 2001.

The numbers are growing fast but the average footprint of an Asian is still seven times smaller than that of a North American and more than three times smaller than that of a European. Per capita footprints of rapidly transforming nations such as China have remained relatively stable over the past eight years, despite huge economic growth, the report found.

"Resource accounting is an opportunity for more effective management of our ecological assets," says Dr. Mathis Wackernagel, executive director of Global Footprint Network, who along with Kadoorie Farm and Botanic Garden (KFGB) partnered the WWF's Asia Pacific 2005 Ecological Footprint and Ecological Wealth Report. "The footprint is not about how bad the situation is, but what we can do about it."

Words & Expressions

devour	vt.	to eat up quickly and hungrily; destroy sth./sb. completely
shape	vt.	to have an important influence on the way that sb./sth. develops
projection	n.	an estimate or a statement of what figures, amounts, or events will be in the future based on what is happening now
sustainability	n.	the use of natural products and energy in a way that does not harm the environment
boom	n.	a sudden increase in trade and economic activity; a period of wealth and success
account for		to be a particular amount or part of sth.
weed... out		to remove or get rid of people or things from a group
scramble	vi.	to manage to achieve sth. with difficulties, or in a hurry, without much control
assume	vt.	to begin to have a particular quality or appearance

Comprehension

1. Please briefly introduce the current situation of natural resource consumption.
2. What does "China can decide if the world moves towards sustainable economic development" mean?
3. Why is China caught in a dilemma according to Paragraph 4?
4. As for foreign investment in China, what changes will take place according to Xing Houyuan?
5. What is indicated from resource accounting?

Translation

Please translate the parts in waves into Chinese.

Questions for Discussion
1. How can China lead Asian countries towards sustainable economic development?
2. What is cleaner investment? How can China lead FDI in a proper way?

Passage

Those Gloating Dismal Scientists
Josef Joffe

Despite political mayhem, the world economy is doing fine. For now let's count our blessings (We'll get to the bad news in a moment.). Economically, the world has not sparkled so brightly in years. Since 2003, the global economy has been expanding at a heartening clip—close to 5% per year, according to the International Monetary Fund, which foresees more good years to come, at least until 2010. Globalization is acting precisely as predicted—as an engine of growth that accelerates investments by leveling borders and speeds up consumption and driving down prices. These competitive pressures also bear down on costs, and so money remains cheap while (core) inflation is safely confined. If US growth has slowed a bit, Japan and Euroland are no longer a drag on the global economy. More significant is the uptick in confidence. Last year, those morose Europeans called off their consumption strike, and so consumer spending is up by around 2%. That may not be very impressive by Chinese standards, but it's downright profligate when compared to the tightfistedness of past years.

What's going on here is a decoupling of the world economy from world politics, where the bad news keeps piling up like the mangled victims of terror and mayhem in Baghdad. Iran, thanks to the weakening of American power, is on a roll, and so is Syria, which less than two years ago was shown the door in Lebanon. The Democratic People's Republic of Korea has exploded a nuclear device, and Russia is back to its imperial ways, except that Putin is much more effective with his pipelines than was the Politburo with its tanks and missiles. Much of Africa is stuck in poverty, war and disease while Latin America is again succumbing to the false promises of populist demagoguery. Last summer's bloody melee in Lebanon, fought against a Hizballah trained and equipped by Tehran, may have been the first Israeli-Iranian war. The Taliban, supposedly crushed in 2001, is doing very nicely in Afghanistan. The war against terror resembles a game of whack-a-mole: beat down one head, and see three more creatures pop out of the other holes.

So here is the paradox of decoupling. On the one hand, Islamist terrorism has imposed a huge transaction tax on the global economy; just try to put a price tag on millions of hours wasted by passengers waiting at security, on container and cargo controls, on cumbersome border checks, on the expansion of police and intelligence personnel—not to speak of the non-monetary costs of civil liberties curtailed. On the other hand, globalization just gallops along. "We told you so," hard-core practitioners of the dismal science might crow. "Economics beats politics any time." The mighty dynamics of expansion seem to beat them out. So does the history of the first globalization, from 1850 – 1914. There were lots of small wars then: the Crimean one, the wars of German unification, a spate of long-forgotten battles over the Balkans, skirmishes from one end of Africa to another and throughout Southeast Asia. Yet international trade and investment prevailed over protectionist sentiment until the big war, that is, World War I, which triggered 70 years of deglobalization—tariff walls, capital controls and autarky. Politics produces those exogenous factors economists always invoke to hedge their optimistic bets, which is why we can't count on the decoupling effect forever.

The obvious candidate for recoupling—for something that reduces the world's economy to the miserable level of its politics—is a preventive strike against Iranian nuclear installations, with all the global repercussions that would imply. Israel might like to launch one, but cannot; the US could do so, but will not, given the debilitating unfinished business in Iraq and Afghanistan. Yet even if a catastrophic war is unlikely, the world remains a dangerous place—made more dangerous by the condition of its prime power. The US today is what Britain was during the first globalization: the anchor of the liberal world order. Those who rightly railed against the US when it threw its weight around and treated its partners with contempt should now mull the question: who is going to take care of the world's political business? China, Russia, or the EU?

Today, the problem is not an overbearing, but a weakened and demoralized America, a giant whose physical power grievously exceeds its authority and legitimacy. Even the hyper-power's rivals must wish that the US would return to the politics of responsibility that the Bush Administration has so willfully ignored. Yes, the world economy is doing very nicely. But there are too many exogenous factors out there that can turn into short fuses. The best hope is for a US company that will again temper raw strength with trustworthiness—and which remembers that it has always done best for itself when it did good for the rest of the world.

(Josef Joffe is publisher-editor of the German weekly *Die Zeit* and a fellow at Stanford's Hoover Institution.)

Words & Expressions

mayhem   n.   a state of violent disorder or riotous confusion; havoc

sparkle	vt.	to shine brightly with flashes of light
uptick	n.	a slight rise or rising trend in the stock market
morose	adj.	very unhappy, bad tempered and silent; sullen
profligate	adj.	recklessly extravagant or wasteful
decouple	vt.	to release the link between; disconnect
mangle	vt.	to ruin or spoil through ineptitude or ignorance
demagoguery	n.	impassioned appeals to the prejudices and emotions of the populace
melee	n.	confused hand-to-hand fight or struggle among several people
cumbersome	adj.	slow and inefficient
curtail	vt.	to cut short or cut off a part of
gallop	vi.	to move or progress swiftly
hard-core	adj.	intensely loyal; die-hard
spate	n.	a sudden, almost overwhelming outpouring
skirmish	n.	a minor short-term fight
autarky	n.	a policy of national self-sufficiency and non-reliance on imports or economic aid
exogenous	adj.	originating from outside; derived externally
repercussion	n.	an often indirect effect or result of some previous action or event
mull	vt.	to go over extensively in the mind; ponder

Comprehension

1. What does the political mayhem refer to in the text?
2. Can you interpret in your own words the paradox of decoupling of the world economy from world politics?
3. Is it true or not that the author agrees with the statement "Economics beats politics any time"? Why?
4. How do you understand "yet even if a catastrophic war is unlikely, the world remains a dangerous place—made more dangerous by the condition of its prime power"?
5. What's the main idea of this text? What does the author really want to tell us?

Translation

Please translate the part in waves into Chinese.

Questions for Discussion

1. What's your comment on "the US today is the anchor of the liberal world order"?
2. Can economy and politics be separated in the process of globalization?

Unit 17

Passage

Five Steps to Prevent Future Energy Woes
Zhou Dadi

Editor's note: At a recent seminar sponsored by China Daily, researchers analyzed the influence of rising global oil prices on China, and gave their appraisals of the country's energy strategy. Here is one opinion:

Conservation should be the top priority in formulating China's mid-and long-term energy strategies.

This is a necessary option dictated by the need for long-term harmonious and sustainable development. This is also based on the consideration of China's reality, reflecting the country's determination to take a new type of approach to industrialization. Broadening the sources of supply and economizing consumption is the way forward.

The Fifth Plenary Session of 16th Central Committee of the Chinese Communist Party (CPC), which was convened recently, made it clear that resource conservation, and energy saving in particular, should be a vitally important aspect of the basic national policy.

In addition, in the CPC Central Committee's proposals for drafting the 11th Five-Year Plan (2006 – 2010), there are only two quantitative development goals. One is that the per capita GDP of the country is set to double by 2010 compared with 2000. The other is that energy volume consumed in turning out a certain unit of GDP should drop by 20 percent. This further shows that the central authorities have put the energy issue very high on the agenda.

Dictated by this, the annual energy saving rate is supposed to reach 4.5 percent, which is a pretty hard task to fulfil. If we manage to achieve this goal, we will set a good example for other developing countries in the course of their industrialization. China simply cannot tread on the footsteps of others in its modernization drive, especially considering the country's specific conditions and the poor prospects of the world energy market.

Per capita energy consumption in China every year is currently 1 ton of standard oil, meaning other forms of energy such as coal and gas are also converted into oil according to their fuel value. But the average energy consumption of developed countries stands at 4 tons. In the United States, however, the per capita energy consumption is 8 tons of standard oil. China, considering its huge population, simply cannot afford that level of consumption.

Our goal is to realize modernization through low per capita energy consumption, which means much lower than the per capita 4-ton standard oil consumption in developed countries.

As a result, we should not regard the growth of GDP as the only indicator to measure our development. Instead, sustainable development and rational energy consumption have become important targets.

First, in order to bring about an energy-saving and environmentally friendly society, we should strengthen energy management and refrain from launching large-scale energy-consuming industrial projects. The central government has decided that 10 major energy-saving projects will be launched during the 11th Five-Year period, bringing in billions of yuan in investment.

At the same time, education on energy saving and publicity campaigns in this regard should be strengthened in order to nurture energy-saving awareness among the general public. Energy frugality is not only a matter of industrial structure, but also a matter that will have great impact on the consumption mode of future Chinese society.

Second, energy-supply sources should be pluralized and the country's own energy resources including coal, petroleum, natural gas, hydraulic power and renewable energy resources should be tapped to the full.

The country burns 2 billion tons of coal yearly and no other form of energy is likely to replace it in the foreseeable future. So we should upgrade the mode of coal burning.

If China's per capita coal consumption volume drops to the level of Europe, we would need to import more than 500 million tons of petroleum each year. This is an impossible burden given the current world oil market.

China currently consumes huge quantities of coal because it has no other choice. What we should do under such circumstances is to efficiently prevent coal mine accidents and pollution caused by coal firing, and use coal more economically.

At the same time, development of nuclear power, hydraulic power and natural gas should be strengthened, as part of the effort to optimize our energy resource mix.

Renewable energy resources need to be tapped so that this kind of energy can play a supporting role and, in turn, help ease energy supply strains.

Third, international cooperation in energy resources is called for. When China goes upstream into the field of international oil and gas exploration, it will help increase the global energy supplies and balance the market. Doing this will also help improve China's ability of withstanding the impacts brought by international oil price fluctuations.

In international co-operation, China should become involved in market competition, and pursue its own interests while avoiding international clashes. Besides, we should help improve the international energy-supply security structure. The current framework cannot be said to be sound and complete. For example, Asian countries do not constitute the focus in this structure, and it also fails to make provisions for developing countries' increasing energy demands.

Fourth, energy-related environmental questions should be dealt with. Besides our country's own energy-related pollution such as atmospheric pollution, we should also address bigger issues such as global warming.

Fifth, energy-related technologies should be developed in a bid to find a long-term solution. This includes energy-saving technologies, and substitution-energy technologies.

We believe that China can resolve the problems it is facing in energy resources, the environment, economics and society's sustainable development in a step-by-step way. We are doing our best to make contributions to the world's energy security while tackling our own energy questions in an overall way.

(The author is director-general of the Energy Research Institute of the National Development and Reform Commission.)

Words & Expressions

dictate	vt.	to prescribe with authority; impose
economize	vt.	to use or manage with thrift
quantitative	adj.	being or capable of being measured by quantity
tread	vi.	to set down the foot or feet in walking; step; walk
convert	vt.	to change into another form, substance, or state, or from one purpose, system, etc. to another
indicator	n.	any of various statistical value that together provide an indication of the condition or direction of the economy
frugality	n.	wise economy in the management of money and other resources
pluralize	vt.	to make sth. become more than one
hydraulic	adj.	of, involving, moved by, or operated by a fluid, especially water, under pressure
tap	vt.	to draw upon; begin to use
withstand	vt.	to resist or oppose, esp. successfully
constitute	vt.	to be the elements or parts of; compose

Comprehension

1. Why can't China simply tread on the footsteps of others in its modernization drive?
2. What does the author mean by the statement "We should not regard the growth of GDP as the only indicator to measure our development."?
3. What kind of role can education play in the sustainable development endeavor?
4. Why is international cooperation in energy resources important for China's sustainable development?
5. What do you think of the five steps to prevent future energy woes?

Translation

Please translate the parts in waves into Chinese.

Questions for Discussion

1. What is long-term harmonious and sustainable development?
2. Which is the right approach to industrialization in China and the world as a whole? Why?

Unit 18

Passage

Green or Gray?
Richard Mullins

Chinese students are getting greener, but some feel they are swimming against the tide.

A rapidly developing China is running up against all kinds of environmental problems, just as today's developed nations did more than a century ago. The difference is that now these problems are occurring on a much greater scale, and they're wreaking far more damage upon the environment. So, as the political and business leaders of tomorrow, or indeed as citizens of China today, how concerned are the country's college students about their environment, and what are they and their universities doing to help prevent its deterioration?

"Sandstorms, desertification, and polluted air, water and land—these are just some examples of environmental deterioration that we face in China today," says a Beijing student Wang Ou. "Are students aware of these things? They would have to be blind not to be." Yet according to www.people.com.cn, a Chinese web portal, just 70 percent of respondents to an environmental survey conducted in Peking University, the country's leading university, said they had a "normal level" of awareness about the issue. They identified the top three sources of environmental harms on their campus as water and electricity wastage, overuse of paper materials, and the use of disposable chopsticks.

"The problems run much deeper than that," says Wang Ou. "I may be cynical, but when I see 1,000 new cars rolling onto the streets of Beijing every day, or canals clogged up with polystyrene food containers every time I get a train out of the city, or read newspaper articles about the latest environmental catastrophe, I am not filled with great hope." Wang feels college students need to take a more proactive role in addressing environmental issues today, because they will be the ones that have to clean up the mess in the years and decades to come.

Universities Are Doing More

At least universities, as the cradle of tomorrow's scientists, businesspeople and government leaders, are taking the issue more seriously these days. Tsinghua University's Development of the Environment has set up a movement called the Green Organization. The highly popular organization arranges plenty of interesting activities that students are happy to take part in, like tree-planting expeditions and organizing recycling campaigns. They get great participation rates—when the students can find the time. There are similar organizations in other Chinese universities, too. These organizations promote environmental awareness among college students, and hope that they will then spread the information farther a field. "Last summer, my classmates and I went out to some local residential areas and handed out leaflets with information on daily actions that every individual can take to reduce his or her burden on the environment," says Wang Ou. "I would say that most of the residents we spoke to were receptive to our ideas. They read our leaflets, and promised to take these small actions. But who knows what they did in practice? Maybe they threw our leaflets on the ground as soon as they got around the corner!"

Others have ventured a little deeper into the field, and returned with more positive experiences. Wang Chuang is a student in Tsinghua University. It is his opinion that "Environmental problems have emerged as a result of China's huge population and rapid development. Most students these days are well aware of this. But they don't know the true situation. They need to actually go to these places, and get more deeply involved, to grasp a realistic idea of the situation, and moreover, of what is being done to fix it." So Wang Chuang did just that—he was part of a research team organized by Tsinghua Unirersity that visited an area of Inner Mongolia Autonomous Region earlier this year to find solutions to environmental problems caused by overgrazing on its once-expansive grasslands.

Wang was one of an 11-member team called the "Green Light". It was made up of students from fields as diverse as electronic engineering, hydroelectricity, and even law. None of the team members had a background in environmental studies, but all of them were concerned and eager to help. Years of overgrazing on the grasslands had devastated the local environment, and team member Zhao Chenlong describes how "Two potential solutions were tested on a small area of land. One was the planting of trees in affected areas; the other was surrounding them with blocks that would prohibit grazing sheep and cattle from entering, in the hope that the situation would remedy itself within five years. When results show which is the best solution, it will be applied to a much wider scale."

The team was charged with the task of researching the "realities" in the local area. Wang Chuang says, "Simply removing the problem, i.e., the grazing sheep, would affect the local people, and that would not have a satisfactory outcome. So we had to carry out thorough research on the shepherds, on their basic needs, and on their lifestyles. We visited them in their homes and examined the local conditions." All the group members then discussed what they had seen, and approached the subject from a number of different angles. "These sessions inspired many new ideas," says Wang Chuang. "It was great to be out in the field together, discussing these and other environmental problems with students from different parts of the country. With so many people willing to discuss the issues, and more importantly, take action, it certainly gave us the feeling that all of these problems can eventually be overcome." The team's final task was to draft a report on its findings, and hand it in to the local government, which would take things from there.

The Debate Goes On

Many of China's pollution problems have emerged in tandem with the country's breakneck economic growth. China naturally has the right—and the duty—to create better opportunities and livelihoods for its citizens. But is the government doing enough to clean up the leftovers? Some students certainly think it is. Zhao Chenlong says, "My home province of Shanxi is a coal-producing area with plenty of heavy industry. It suffered heavily from the effects of pollution in the 1990s, but the government took various measures to address these problems, and things are much better now. And as a citizen of the province, I can say that economic development is crucial to our people. Finding a balance between that and environmental protection is the objective, but it is no easy task. I am confident that we are going in the right direction."

Not everyone shares Zhao's confidence. Wang Ou says, "I doubt very much that the government is doing all it can to solve the country's pollution problems. Take Beijing, the Chinese capital, for example. There are less than two years to go until the Olympic Games come to this city. This event is one of the most important things that the government has been working on this decade, yet look out your window, and the air is still thick with pollution. If we're not making enough efforts to solve the problems here in the capital, where the eyes of the world will be fixed in 2008, I doubt very much if sufficient efforts are being made to bring pollution under control on other cities around the country."

One thing that is not likely to run out of fuel anytime soon is debate on the environment. Whether that's taking place between signatories and non-signatories to the Kyoto Protocol on Climate Change, or between a couple of sweepers on the street, it's an issue that every human being is—or should be—concerned about. Young Chinese people are genuinely worried about the effects that pollutants have on their health, and that of their future children. "Economic development is a good thing for our country," says Wang Ou, "I do not doubt that. But should it come at such a high price? We breathe poisoned air. We eat poisoned vegetables. I am not optimistic about the future." But another "Green Light" member, Wu Tianyi, says, "We cannot go backwards. We must have faith that those in charge will find the right balance between economic development and environmental protection." Watch the space outside your window for more ...

Words & Expressions

wreak	vt.	to cause to happen or to occur as a consequence
desertification	n.	the gradual transformation of habitable land into desert; be usually caused by climate change or by destructive use of the land
polystyrene	n.	a polymer of styrene; a rigid transparent thermoplastic
catastrophe	n.	a state of extreme (usually irremediable) ruin and misfortune
venture	vi.	to proceed somewhere despite the risk of possible dangers
hydroelectricity	n.	electricity produced by water power
remedy	vt.	to provide relief for; set straight or right
in tandem (with)		arranged one behind the other; together, in partnership
breakneck	adj.	moving at very high and dangerous speed

Comprehension

1. Cite some examples of environmental deterioration that we face in China today.
2. What are the functions of the Green Organization and other similar organizations?
3. How did the "Green Light" do their research? Did they get anywhere?
4. What are the effects that pollutants have on human beings?
5. Are you optimistic about the future of our environment? And why?

Translation

Please translate the parts in waves into Chinese.

Questions for Discussion

1. Talk about the causes of China's current environmental problems.
2. How to strike a balance between economic growth and environmental protection?

Unit 19

Passage

Recycling Big
Zhang Kuo

A grand ceremony was held on May 31 this year to mark the opening of the China Qingyuan Recycling Resource Demonstration Base in Guangdong Province's Qingyuan City. The base was established after winning approval from the State Development and Reform Commission, the Ministry of Commerce, the State Environmental Protection Administration and three other relevant ministries. It reflects China's efforts in constructing a recyclable economy. The base is also a provincial-level demonstration program for building an energy- and resource-saving society and part of the Ministry of Commerce's endeavors to build a modern recycling industry system. So what is the current situation of China's recycling industry? And where does Qingyuan fit in? Guan Aiguo, president of the Qingyuan base, explains.

China's Recycling Industry

Renewable resources refer to so-called waste materials generated in the course of daily life or manufacturing that have degraded in value but can be recycled and re-used. Substituting these resources for primary raw materials reduces energy consumption and pollution levels. It is hence little wonder that the recycling industry, as the most important step in the development of a recyclable economy, has received strong support from governments around the world.

Here in China, renewable resources have proven vital to some major industries. They account for 26 percent of raw materials consumed by the steel industry, more than 20 percent of those used in the non-ferrous metals industry, and some 50 percent of those used in the papermaking industry.

Yet China's recycling industry remains in its infancy, and teething problems abound. They include the low quality of labor, small-scale operation, a yawning technological gap, secondary pollution and a low processing ratio. Prior to 2001, there were only 5,000 to 6,000 recycling businesses nationwide. But when the government abolished the waste collection certification system and formulated special tax policies in 2002, the number of recycling enterprises exploded, particularly in the coastal areas of Southeast China, employing more than 10 million people.

Despite the industry's being largely propelled by government policies, poor regulations and management caused chaos in its operation. A series of problems emerged for society, the environment and public facilities. Motivated by profit alone, most of the small-scale operators produced even more secondary pollution and waste.

The Qingyuan Demonstration Base

The recycling industry in Qingyuan City has a history of 20 years. Since its inception, it has grown into a large-scale industry with local characteristics and excellent reputation for collecting, dismantling and processing waste materials.

Some RMB 1.5 billion has been invested in the China Qingyuan Recycling Resource Demonstration Base, invested and operated by the Qingyuan Huaqing Recycling Resource Investment and Development Co., Ltd, which was co-founded by the China Renewable Resources Development Company and the Guangdong Xinyaguang Electrical Cable Co., Ltd.

After all the projects are completed, the base will be the largest renewable resources collecting, dismantling and processing factory in the world. It will have the capacity to handle 3 million tons of waste hardware, electrical appliances, motors, electric wires, cables, metals and plastics, and produce RMB 50 million worth of recycled industrial raw materials every year. The first-phase construction, now completed, covers 50 hectares of land.

Featuring unified planning, lawful operations and the implementation of a unified policy, the base is the first in China's recycling industry to boast modernized management with a platform for the exchange of information, labor, logistics, trade, technology and capital. It has centralized sewage and waste treatment plants, and leads the way in training its technicians and workers.

Most recycling enterprises are still small-scale operations with disintegrated management systems. The Qingyuan mode is the exact opposite. And in terms of reducing energy consumption, increasing the processing ratio and reducing secondary pollution, the base is considered a model for others to follow.

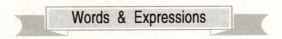

demonstration program	program that shows and explains how sth. works
renewable resources	any natural resource (as wood or solar energy) that can be replenished naturally with the passage of time

recycling	n.	the act of processing used or abandoned materials for use in creating new products
teething problems	n.	troubles which occur in the early stages of doing sth. new
certification	n.	confirmation that some fact or statement is true
propel	vt.	to cause to move forward with force
inception	n.	an event that is a beginning; a first part or stage of subsequent events
dismantle	vt.	to take apart; disassemble; tear down

Comprehension

1. What do renewable resources refer to? And what is their importance to major industries?
2. What's the relationship between the recycling industry and recyclable economy?
3. Which phase has China's recycling industry developed into? What kinds of problems has it faced?
4. What's the scale of the Qingyuan demonstration base after it is completed?
5. Can you say something about the characteristics in management of Qingyuan demonstration base?

Translation

Please translate the parts in waves into Chinese.

Questions for Discussion

1. What is "recyclable economy"? Why is it important to China's development?
2. Do you believe that there are barriers to achieving the recyclable economy currently? If so, what are they?

Passage

Forex Rate Forming Mechanism Reformed

Zhang Dingmin

China announced a further move to reform its exchange rate forming mechanism yesterday, introducing an internationally prevalent price-finding mechanism in the interbank foreign exchange market.

The introduction of OTC (over-the-counter) transactions will improve the exchange rate transmission mechanism and help meet businesses' risk-hedging needs. But it will not broaden fluctuations of the renminbi exchange rate, the central bank said.

"With a view to improving the managed floating exchange rate regime based on market supply and demand with reference to a basket of currencies, promoting development of the foreign exchange market, diversifying the mode of foreign exchange transactions, and strengthening the pricing capability of the financial institutions, OTC transactions will be introduced in the interbank spot forex market starting today," the People's Bank of China (PBOC) said in a statement.

Participants in the interbank forex market now will be able to engage in forex transactions either based on centralized credit authorization and price bidding, or the new OTC market, which is based on bilateral credit authorization and settlement.

The system of market makers that are obliged to quote both selling and buying prices are introduced at the same time to provide liquidity.

The new OTC market will deepen the forex market so as to lay a solid foundation for improving the formation mechanism of the renminbi exchange rate, and enhance the representativeness of the central parity of the Chinese currency in the new market structure.

This is because the prices quoted by market makers reflect not only their expectations of daily purchases and sales of forex and positions resulted from market making transactions, but also their judgments of movements in the international market, the central bank said.

It will also help enhance the core competitiveness of financial institutions, particularly market makers, and encourage them to provide a richer variety of exchange rate risk management tools for businesses and households, the central bank said.

"After the exchange rate reform, the central bank will have to provide hedging tools to be able to execute a managed floating exchange rate system," said Zhang Xuechun, an economist with the Asian Development Bank.

After its landmark reform on July 21 last year that let the renminbi appreciate by 2 percent to US dollar and linked the currency to a basket of currencies instead of the US dollar, China has taken a slew of measures to establish a market-oriented exchange rate formation mechanism, including the launch of risk-hedging tools like forwards and swaps.

"The next natural move could be the broadening of participants of OTC transactions," she said, noting that the OTC market is still confined to the interbank market, where only financial institutions are allowed.

The central bank said the renminbi exchange rate will unlikely experience larger fluctuations after the new method is adopted to form the central parity, stressing that the floating bank of the renminbi exchange rate remain unchanged.

The central parity of the renminbi against US dollar, based on which banks quote their prices, will now be decided on the weighted average of prices from all market makers, after excluding the highest and lowest offers.

The central parity of renminbi against the euro, the Japanese yen and Hong Kong dollar will be determined by the renminbi-US dollar central parity and the exchange rates of those currencies against the US dollar in the international market.

Words & Expressions

forex	n.	[<FOR(EIGN) + EX(CHANGE)]
hedging	n.	strategy used to offset business or investment risk
spot market		cash market; commodities market in which goods are sold for cash and delivered immediately
credit authorization		a check on credit standing (before credit extension) to avoid possible credit fraud
price bidding		buying offer
parity	n.	the state of being equal, of having equality of value or importance
position	n.	bank's net balance in a foreign currency
appreciate	vi.	to increase in value
forwards	n.	actual purchase or sale of a specific quantity of foreign

		currency, or other financial instrument at a price specified now, with delivery and settlement at a specified future date
swap	n.	arrangement under which one foreign currency is exchanged for another
weighted average		in statistical calculations, an arithmetical mean that gives each item its proper weight or importance

Comprehension
1. What is the exchange rate reform?
2. According to the PBOC, what is the purpose of the introduction of OTC?
3. What do the prices quoted by market makers reflect?
4. What differences will OTC market make?
5. What will happen to the renminbi after the new method is adopted?

Translation
Please translate the parts in waves into Chinese.

Questions for Discussion
1. How will OTC work in China's exchange market?
2. Recently, foreign exchange reserve has been increasing so fast in China, what's your attitude towards this phenomenon?

Unit 21

Passage

Money Supply Target Lowered
Feng Jie

Bank promises to continue RMB exchange rate mechanism reform.

China's central bank has announced a slightly lower growth target for the money supply for this year, maintaining a prudent monetary policy stance as the economy continues on its rapid growth path.

The People's Bank of China (PBOC) also pledged to press ahead with reforming the renminbi exchange rate mechanism to let market demand and supply play a fundamental role in determining the exchange rate.

The growth target of the broad money supply M2, which covers cash in circulation and all deposits, and largely reflects the potential purchasing power in the entire economy, is set at 16 percent for this year, the bank said. The target is lower than 2005's 17 percent, which was revised up from 15 percent at the beginning of last year as real growth outpaced expectations. The growth rate was 18.3 percent at the end of November.

"It indicates the central bank still wants to keep its control of money and has no intention to get expansive," said Li Ruoyu, an analyst with the State Information Centre. "It is still emphasizing prudence."

Li's centre projects a higher 17 percent growth rate for M2, which she said partly reflects the tendency of slower circulation of money in the economy. A slew of factors indicate that slower money supply growth is achievable this year.

The exchange rate reform and a foreign trade policy, which are aiming to reduce surpluses, are expected to take away some pressure on the central bank to release new money to mop up excess US dollars in the marketplace, she said.

The huge inflows of foreign exchange resulting from surpluses in China's balance of payment have been forcing the PBOC to release new money into the banking system in the past two years, as it purchased excess dollars to enforce a floating band for the renminbi.

Greater flexibility for the exchange rate mechanism, which was achieved in a major reform on July 21 last year by linking the currency to a basket of foreign currencies, has helped reduce the pressure, analysts said.

The stronger restraint on commercial banks' impulse to lend, as a result of stricter requirements on capital adequacy, is another factor reining in loan growth, which drives money supply growth, Li said.

The widely perceived possibility of a rebound in the growth rate of fixed investment also justifies a slower growth of money supply. The rapid growth of fixed investment, which was expected to drop to 25 percent for the whole of last year from levels as high as 50 percent, was a major reason for worries about the Chinese economy overheating.

"Monetary policy has to be somewhat accommodative, since a tightening in credit will likely cause liquidity difficulties in businesses that are suffering from overcapacity," Li said.

Government officials have said overcapacity is already plaguing sectors like steel and car making, largely as a result of over-investment, while some other sectors, like cement and textiles, are showing early signs of this trend.

The PBOC said yesterday it would continue to improve the renminbi exchange rate mechanism, trying to let market forces play a fundamental role, but did not elaborate.

In a statement yesterday, the State Administration of Foreign Exchange (SAFE) pledged to take further steps this year to promote the development of the foreign exchange market, the basis for achieving the State's goal of building a market-driven exchange rate system.

The administration also said supervision of short-term debts will be strengthened, and regulations governing financial institutions' offshore businesses will be formulated to prevent speculative funds from entering China.

Words & Expressions

prudent	adj.	careful and sensible; marked by sound judgment
pledge	vt.	to promise solemnly and formally
outpace	vt.	to surpass or outdo (another), as in speed, growth, or performance
project	vt.	to calculate, estimate, or predict (something in the future), based on present data or trends
mop up		to absorb
liquidity	n.	being in cash or easily convertible to cash; debt paying ability
overcapacity	n.	too great a capacity for production of commodities or delivery of services in relation to actual need

| offshore | adj. | located or based in a foreign country and not subject to tax laws |
| speculative | adj. | engaging in, given to, or involving financial speculation |

Comprehension

1. What is M2?
2. Should market play a fundamental role in determining the exchange rate? Why?
3. Why are the exchange rate reform and a foreign trade policy expected?
4. How many reasons does the author give in order to justify a slower growth of money supply?
5. What kind of result can overcapacity lead to?

Translation

Please translate the parts in waves into Chinese.

Questions for Discussion

1. How did Chinese economy overheating happen in 2005? What measures did the government take to curb overheating of the economy?
2. Why does China maintain a prudent monetary policy this year?

Passage

Strategy in the Knowledge Economy
W. Chan Kim & Renee Mauborgne

At the heart of most strategic thinking is competition. Yet strategy driven by competition usually has three unintended effects:
- Imitative, not innovative, approaches to the market.
- Companies act reactively.
- A company's understanding of emerging mass markets and changing customer demands become hazy.

The reason is that when asked to build competitive advantage most managers look at what their competitors are doing and then seek to do it better. In other words, their strategic thinking regresses towards the competition. As a result, companies often achieve no more than an incremental improvement on what the competition is doing—imitation, not innovation.

For the past 10 years we have looked at companies that have recorded ongoing and high levels of growth and profits compared to their competitors. The strategies they have followed are what we call "value innovation". This is fundamentally different from adding layers of competitive advantage or trying to outperform competitors. Value innovation focuses on offering quantum leaps in value for customers. The key is the simultaneous pursuit of radically superior value and lower costs.

Starbucks, Virgin Atlantic, Enron, Bloomberg, Home Depot, Wal-Mart and others are examples of companies that have succeeded by consistently focusing their innovative efforts on customer value and lower costs.

Value innovation places an equal emphasis on both value and innovation. Value with no innovation stresses improving the net benefit to the customer or value creation. Innovation with no value can be too technology-driven. Value innovation grounds innovation in buyer value.

While innovation itself may be random, value innovation is not. It deliberately seeks quantum leaps in customer value.

There are five key ways in that value innovation differs from conventional strategic logic:
1. While many companies may allow industry conditions to dictate what is possible, probable and profitable, value innovators see their industries as inherently malleable and challenge the inevitability of industry conditions.
2. While the orthodox strategy may be to focus on outpacing the competition, value innovators aim to dominate the market by introducing a major advance in buyer value that makes the competition irrelevant.
3. Traditionally, companies focus on customer segmentation, customization and retention. But value innovators seek key value commonalties that will allow them to capture the mass market even if they have to lose some customers.
4. Most companies start by more fully exploiting their existing key assets and capabilities; while value innovators do the same, they are not constrained by them. They are willing to tear sown and rebuild if necessary.
5. Conventional companies concentrate on improving traditional industry products and services. Value innovators think in terms of total customer solution, even if this means going outside traditional industry boundaries.

Thus value innovation differs from traditional strategy in both the height of its ambitions and the breadth of the way it defines customers. The focus on incremental improvements slips to the background and it identifies its target market not merely as its own or its competitors' customers. It also seeks to pull in buyers that have never patronized an industry. Companies may often look to their customers for inspiration, but the best ideas often come from listening to competitors' customers and people who are not even, as yet, in your market.

For example, in 1991 US club manufacturer Callaway Golf launched the "Big Bertha" club. The product soon dominated the market, taking increased market share and, more importantly, growing the total market. The reason is that in highly competitive market Callaway did not focus on the competition. Rivals had fiercely benchmarked each other, resulting in very similar clubs with over-sophisticated enhancements. Callaway looked at why in the "country club" market, more people played tennis than golf. The answer was that small club head made it easier and more fun, attracting both existing and new players. Callaway Golf did not look at how it might beat other golf club manufacturers by offering an improved solution to the traditional goal—how to fit a golf ball further. Instead it looked at offering a solution to a customer problem—how to hit a golf ball more easily. By redefining the problem in this way Callaway grew the market by attracting customers who previously had not wished to play golf.

Value innovators seek to create new and superior value. A conventional focus on retaining and better satisfying existing customers promotes a fear of challenging the status quo. Value innovators monitor existing customers but also pursue non-customers.

The conventional strategic objective is to gain a competitive advantage by offering improvements against industry benchmarks. But this type of benchmarking is not what value innovation is all about. Value innovation changes industries. For example, Bloomberg's value innovation leapfrogged existing market leaders to redefine an industry. Reuters and Dow Jones' Telerate were providing online stock price data. Bloomberg offered smart terminals capable of data analysis that allowed traders and analysts to make decisions more quickly and accurately, allowing it to rapidly become the market leader and leave the others in the dust.

Note, though, that while value innovation is the essence of strategy in the knowledge economy, it is not enough on its own. Any strategy that attracts customers will be copied. Value innovators therefore also need to deploy the tactics that traditionally preserve the first mover's advantage, and often these will be incremental improvements to the original value innovation. In this respect, value innovation produces a punctuated equilibrium—major change followed by periods of refinement and consolidation.

When they find superior value, value innovators deploy capabilities that exist both within and outside their companies to exploit it. Value innovators frequently have a network of partners that provide complementary assets and capabilities.

For example, SMH, creator of the Swatch, had no expertise in the mass watch market, in plastics mounding or even in design. It did have an idea of superior value—the wristwatch as a fashion accessory—plus the insight to create, buy or borrow the expertise needed to produce it.

To make value innovation a reality companies have to go beyond conventional competence-based thinking that takes an inside-out approach and ask, what would we do if we were to start anew? That opens the creative scope and range of opportunities that companies consider.

Quantum leaps in value almost involve major changes in behaviour and working practices. These will not be achieved without people willingly cooperate with the innovation process and making their skills and experience available to a company.

But the key to gaining this willing cooperation is the idea of "fair process".

Exercising "fair process"—fairness in the process of making and executing decisions—is a powerful way to recognize people's intellectual and emotional worth. Fair process promotes trust and commitment whereas treatment perceived as unfair makes people hoard their ideas and drag their feet.

Fair process involves three basic principles:
- **Engagement**: involving people in decisions that affect them by seeking their ideas and allowing them to challenge the ideas and assumptions of others.
- **Explanation**: everyone involved or affected should understand the reasons for decisions and why their ideas were accepted or rejected.

- **Establishing clear expectation**: people must know what the objectives are, how their performance will be judged and who is responsible for what.

Fair process and value innovation create a positively reinforcing cycle. Success in value innovation strategy that results from fair process strengthens the group and increases people's belief in the process, thus perpetuating the collaborative and creative models that are the basis of value innovation.

Most companies strive to deliver fair outcomes but do not distinguish this from fair process. Fair outcomes ensure that individuals receive the resources they need or material rewards in exchange for cooperation. But to induce knowledge creation and voluntary cooperation between individuals companies must go beyond fair outcomes to fair process.

Fair process is often not easy for managers. It forces them to be candid and to explain themselves. Just rewards are important, but people are also concerned with how they are treated. If people feel respected and think that decision-making processes are fair they will accept decisions even if they don't benefit from them. Fair process creates an objective, meritocratic culture based on a belief in the intellectual and emotional worth of all employees.

People possessing knowledge are the key resource of companies that follow value innovation strategies. But this resource is increasingly independent and mobile. To capture it, companies must meet expectations of both fair outcome and fair process.

Words & Expressions

hazy	adj.	rather confused; uncertain
regress	vi.	to return to an earlier or less advanced form or state
quantum leap		sudden progress; breakthrough
malleable	adj.	easily influenced or changed
incremental	adj.	increasing gradually by regular degrees or additions
benchmark	vt.	to measure the quality of sth. by comparing it with sth. else of an accepted standard
the status quo		(from Latin) the situation as it is now, or as it was before a recent change
leapfrog	vt.	to get to a higher position or rank by going past sb. else or by missing out some stages
deploy	vt.	to use sth. effectively
accessory	n.	a thing that you can wear or carry that matches your clothes
hoard	vt.	to collect and keep sth. especially secretly
perpetuate	vt.	to make sth. such as a bad situation, a belief, etc.

		continue for a long time
meritocratic	*adj.*	characterized by meritocracy; of or pertaining to meritocrats or meritocracy

Comprehension

1. What are the effects of strategy driven by competition? Please try to explain them one by one.
2. How much do you know about value innovation?
3. What are differences between value innovation and conventional strategic logic?
4. What is fair process? What does it involve?
5. Please explain differences between fair process and fair outcome?

Translation

Please translate the parts in waves into Chinese.

Questions for Discussion

1. What should be the proper strategy when facing competition in the knowledge economy?
2. How can a company achieve value innovation in the knowledge economy?

Unit 23

Passage

The Communication Advantage
Paul A. Argenti & Janis Foreman

Paul A. D. J. Argenti and Janis Foreman explain why following the teachings of Aristotle can help involve key organizational constituencies in helping formulate and implement strategy.

Since the 1970s numerous studies have identified how organizations develop their strategies and, in some instances, how they succeed or fail when moving from a formulated strategy to its implementation. Some of these studies also discuss the importance of communication to the process of implementing strategy, but none of them considers communication to be a central focus. Even studies of strategic implementation make communication a peripheral concern, focusing instead on issues such as organizational structures and processes, reward systems and resource allocation. Despite the importance of these issues, the lack of focus on communication leaves a significant gap in managers' understanding of how to move from formulating to implementing strategy.

So how can senior management use communication effectively to formulate a strategy and to ensure that strategy is implemented?

Unlikely as it may seem, let's turn to the ancient Greek philosopher Aristotle and his work *On Rhetoric* to see the theoretical basis for bridging the gap between strategy and communication. We can use Aristotle's constituency-focused approach to persuasion as a departure point for building a communication framework that can be used by "expressive organizations". These organizations risk expressing their values in the marketplace to attract and form relationships with varied constituencies on which both their survival and success ultimately depend.

In Aristotle's day, the fourth century BC, the fundamental unit of organizational life was the city state, in his case Athens. But despite the historical and cultural gap between our own and Aristotle's time, *On Rhetoric* contains two important elements that inform our understanding of how expressive organizations can effectively design and communicate their vision statements and strategic plans.

The first of these is Aristotle's notion of "deliberative rhetoric", or speeches made in political assemblies where debate occurs for or against a particular kind of future for an organization—in Aristotle's case the city state, and in ours the expressive organization. The second element is his constituency-focused approach to communication—that is, the centrality of the audience to persuasive discourse.

In today's expressive organization, deliberative rhetoric is most akin to the discourse of strategy formulation and implementation. For example, the whole idea behind Gary Hamel's notion of "strategic revolution" is to postulate a future and move constituencies towards it. Under the leadership of CEO Arthur Martinez, Sears, Roebuck and Company put his idea into motion by developing a new vision statement in the mid-1990s—to be internalized by its constituencies—that was hallmark of the company's huge transformation.

In *On Rhetoric* Aristotle used a constituency-focused approach to consider the individual speaker persuading others to think or act according to the speaker's agenda. Aristotle grants a central role to the audience as judges—not merely spectators or recipients—of a particular argument. We have adapted this approach to look at the communication challenges that expressive organizations and their chief spokespeople face as they attempt to formulate and implement strategy.

Each element of the framework—the organization, its messages, its constituencies and its constituency responses—focuses attention on specific challenges for implementing strategy successfully. The organization must determine its objectives for a particular communication with each constituency (What does the organization want each constituency to do?); evaluate the resources available to accomplish the task (What kind of money, human resources and time does the organization have available?); and determine the organization's overall reputation (How does each constituency receive the organization?).

A good way to see the benefits of a constituency-focused approach to formulating and communicating strategy is to examine an organization that employs such an approach, such as Navistar.

Although CEO John Horne of Navistar—a heavy truck manufacturer headquartered in Chicago—did not formally design and use such an approach, his ideas about communication evolved to clearly illustrate his focus:persuading the company's multiple constituencies to help formulate and implement the organization's strategy.

When Horne took over as CEO in 1993 he recognized that the company had significant problems with its constituencies—employees, unions, senior management, the financial community and the media. The company was plagued with a history of union conflict, including a long strike in the 1970s. In turn, the general discontent of the workforce made investors lose confidence in the company's ability to prosper.

Believing that he had to bring his employees on board before raising the confidence of the financial community, Horne supported early initiatives to gather information from employees about their concerns. He used a three-pronged approach: extensive plant visits; an employee survey with follow-up; and direct involvement of union representatives in employee issues.

The dialogue established between senior management and plant employees became so successful in raising morale and in formulating strategy that plant visits became a formalized communication practice by the autumn of 1996. As a result, each month a member of the senior management group visits every plant. Meetings include the senior manager and 30 or 40 employees representing a cross-section of the plant. Senior management brings back what they learn at the plant and, in this way, the employees' voices are brought into top management's discussion of strategy. This continuing discussion has allowed the company to create its message collaboratively with this constituency, a role for communication that Aristotle envisaged long ago in his study of rhetoric.

Navistar's communication group extended this collaboration with employees by conducting extensive employee research to design an employee survey. Survey results, which were presented jointly by management and union leaders and published in newsletters, became the basis for action plans.

The CEO also initiated and maintained dialogue with another vital constituency, union representatives. Union members have been invited to join education and training committees and to recommend changes in this aspect of employee life.

Along with plant employees and union representatives, Horne also targeted senior management as a key internal constituency with which he wanted to improve communications. He instituted a "leadership conference" in 1995, a three-day meeting for the top 550 managers in the firm. On the first day he learned that only 24 percent of the top executives knew that the company had a strategy. By the end of the conference, 98 percent knew. Leadership conferences continue to be a permanent component of the company's approach to communication.

When the company turned its attention to the external world, its first concern was understandably with its customers. Customers focus is, in fact, one of the core values it espouses. Since Horne became CEO, the company has taken actions to revitalize this core value—researching customers' overall experience and expectations of the brand, rethinking each target market group, holding press conferences and giving speeches at industry events to project Navistar as an industry leader. Among other things, the company has also worked to extend its brand image beyond that of "reliability" and "durability" qualities that customers identified—to also include technological leadership and excellence for its extensive distribution network.

To address the skepticism of another external constituency, the financial community, about Navistar's ability to resolve its union problems, senior management developed a powerful, consistent story about how the company was going to solve its difficulties. They decided that, although management would take the blame for the problems, the company needed the employees to work collaboratively with them to help solve them.

As for the media—another key constituency—Horne persisted in opening up a dialogue with them even in the face of media stories that exacerbated the strife between unions and management and resulted in low morale in the plants. Despite initial lack of trust on both sides, the CEO's willingness to respond to questions and his ability to present a consistent story about the company's strategy gradually improved media relations.

As a result of Horne's constituency-focused approach to communication he has been able to change the image of the company, raise employee morale, and improve its overall reputation and financial status.

Given these effects on an organization's image, morale, reputation and bottom line, public interest in rhetoric still pervades today. In the 4th century BC, Aristotle's work grew up alongside Athenian democracy and its need for public debate in the contested arenas of the law courts or public assemblies where issues of great consequence to the individual or the state were decided. Today, however, expensive organizations face other, but no less compelling, challenges:the need to influence and motivate key constituencies and to engage them in formulating as well as implementing strategy.

Words & Expressions

peripheral	adj.	related to the key issue but not of central importance
constituency	n.	a group of supporters or patrons
deliberative	adj.	involved in or characterized by deliberation and discussion and examination
assembly	n.	a group of persons gathered together for a common purpose
postulate	vt.	to put (sth.) forward as a fact or accept (sth.) as true, esp. as a basis for reasoning or argument
akin	adj.	similar or related in quality or character
hallmark	n.	a distinctive characteristic or attribute
plague	vt.	to cause trouble or difficulty to (sb./sth.)
prosper	vi.	to grow stronger; gain in wealth
envisage	vt.	to conceive an image or a picture of, especially as a future possibility
collaboration	n.	act of working jointly
institute	vt.	to initiate; begin
espouse	vt.	to give one's loyalty or support to (a cause, theory, etc.)

Comprehension

1. How did studies of strategic implementation since the 1970s view communication? What did they focus on?
2. Why does the author mention the ancient Greek philosopher Aristotle and his work *On Rhetoric* in the text?
3. What does the author mean by "expressive organizations"?
4. What is Aristotle's "constituency-focused approach"? How has it been made use of by expressive organizations?
5. Can you summarize in your own words how Horne successfully applied constituency focused approach to formulating and communicating strategy as the CEO of Navistar?

Translation

Please translate the parts in waves into Chinese.

Questions for Discussion

1. Can Aristotle's constituency-focused approach work in all kinds of organizations?
2. How much do you know about non-verbal communication? Is it of much importance in business?

Passage

The Revolution in Risk Management
Anthony M. Santomero

Anthony M. Santomero explains why corporations need to manage risk and outlines risk management policy.

Corporate managers are interested both in expected profitability and the risk, or the variability, of reported earnings. This concern is rationalized, or explained, by the existence of costs that vary across the range of possible profit figures associated with any given expected performance. Therefore, the firm is led to treat the variability of earnings as a decision variable that it selects, subject to the usual constraints on management.

How it proceeds to manage the risk position of its activity—how risks are being managed—is the area of concern here.

The question is easy enough. The answer is more difficult.

The area of risk management can be divided into three sub-fields. While there are overlaps, the questions, answers and open issues vary by area of discussion. It is, therefore, useful to address each of the following questions in turn:
- How should risks be managed?
- What have non-financial firms done by way of risk management?
- How have financial firms addressed the issue?

The three areas can be seen as two separate problems: theory and application. However, in as much as financial firm risk management has developed somewhat separately, it is useful to treat the application of risk management techniques in the financial sector as a separate issue.

This first question is the easiest to answer but hard to implement. To the extent that a firm's manager is making the decision to further advance his or her own best interests the problem becomes the usual one of portfolio choice.

Projects and/or activities are selected using the standard risk-return trade-off that finance has long promulgated. Projects are selected according to their expected profitability, their variance and the covariance of their returns with other projects within the firm.

On the other hand, if the manager's concern over risk is due to its effect on overall firm value, then managers must recognize the effect of volatility on market value. This will lead them to alter their decisions and encourage risk management and control.

In either case, implementing such a risk-management procedure requires a strategy that includes both risk identification and risk reduction. The former involves an analysis of the drivers of firm performance and the reasons for the volatility in earnings and/or market value. The latter is accomplished through the use of standard procedures of risk reduction, such as standard diversification procedures, as well as the establishment of rules that limit potential extreme downside results.

From theory to practice, we move from the neat realm of concept into the difficult area of actual implementation. Here, little information exists on the practices currently employed by non-financial firms. General management practices to dampen the variability of cash flow and/or profitability are not documented in any systematic way.

Nonetheless, it is generally accepted that risk management can be conducted in two distinct ways. Either a firm can engage in activities that together result in less volatility than they would exhibit individually or it can engage in financial transactions that will have a similar effect.

The first approach is to embark upon a diversification strategy in the portfolio of businesses operated by the firm—in short, engage in diversification by conglomerate merger. However, conglomerate activity, while once a popular strategy recommended and pursued in the industrial sector, has fallen out of favor. Most firms have learned that they do not necessarily have value-added expertise in more than one area and have found it hard to prosper across industry lines.

As a result, firms concerned about the volatility of earnings have turned to the financial markets. This is because these markets have developed more direct approaches to risk management that transcend the need to invest directly in activities that reduce volatility.

Financial risk management, using financial products such as swaps, options and futures, can accomplish these same ends and has experienced explosive growth. Together, these derivative products have proved to be an important means of risk trading.

In many respects the story associated with risk management for industrial firms is transferable to their financial counterparts. However, the issue is somewhat more complicated for financial firms.

These firms deal in financial markets, as principals and agents, and have a long history of both hedging capability and taking positive risk positions. In fact, it could be argued that their franchise involves taking the financial risk from the non-financial sector.

However, taking financial risk does not imply keeping it. As corporate entities, these organizations, like their non-financial counterparts, must deal with the same issues that motivate the rest of the private sector.

While it could be argued that the existence of regulatory oversight and its implicit guarantee makes these firms less risk averse, the existence of regulators that charter and sustain the institution's franchise makes risk a real issue of concern.

Management, therefore, must find the correct place for risk management in a sector that has both a reason for taking financial risk and reasons for concern over doing so.

For this purpose, it is useful to distinguish two ways of delivering financial services. These can be provided either as an agent or as a principal. In the former, risk is borne by the two sides of the transaction, with little remaining with the financial institution that facilitated it. In the latter, risk is absorbed by the financial institution itself because it places its balance sheet between the two sides of the transaction.

The choice between these two techniques seems to depend upon the institution's value-added or unique expertise in managing the associated risk. For some risks, the institution frequently finds itself in the position of absorbing risk associated with its asset services rather than transferring it while for others the opposite is true.

Empirically, the latter group, where financial transactions transfer risk to the buyer of assets, is growing more rapidly. As information and transaction costs have declined, the fraction of financial assets held by risk-transferring institutions such as mutual funds, pension funds and various unit trusts has increased relative to those held in risk-absorbing institutions such as commercial banks and other depositories. This is due to the decline in the returns offered to these institutions to bear such risks.

Nonetheless, balance sheet risk management is still an important issue in the financial sector. For those institutions that do accept certain types of financial risk, because of their chosen business strategy, risk control and management procedures are essential.

Conceptually, these should involve the same steps and obtain the same results as indicated above. The drivers of uncertainty must be identified and risk reduction strategies outlined. The distinction here is that the risks are somewhat different than those facing the non-financial sector.

The fact that risk matters is, perhaps, not news to senior managers. However, the news is that there is a better understanding of why risk matters and how it should be managed.

Whether a firm is in the manufacturing sector or financial services, it has risks that need to be managed. In today's business environment no organization is immune from risk and none can be without a risk-management and control process.

With the advent of financial change and asset innovation, we have begun to develop a deep understanding of how to fashion an appropriate risk management system. In fact, the implementation of broad risk management systems has become big business—indeed a growth area of management interest and management consulting.

What does such a system involve?

As noted above, it begins with a careful identification of the causes of volatility—the factors that lead to variation in performance.

Next, the risks that have been so identified must be actively managed. Recent research has shown how this is accomplished by the establishment of standardized procedures that measure, monitor and limit the risk-taking activity of firm so as to reduce the volatility of performance. Such systems usually include four parts:

- Standards and reports, which identify, measure and monitor the factors that cause volatility.
- Limits and controls on each of the factors and on each member of the organization that adds risk to the firm's performance profile.
- Guidelines and management recommendations concerning appropriate current exposure to these same risks.
- Accountability and compensation programmes that lead mid-level mangers to take the process seriously.

Shareholders care about risk, the stock market cares and, as has been said, so should senior management. The challenge for these same managers is to embed a risk control system within their organization so as to reduce the volatility of profitability and engender a risk control mentality throughout the organization.

Words & Expressions

overlap	n.	a shared area of interest, knowledge, responsibility, etc.
portfolio	n.	(finance) a set of shares owned by a particular person or organization
trade-off	n.	the act of balancing two things that you need or want but which are opposed to each other
promulgate	vt.	to spread an idea, a belief, etc. among many people
covariance	n.	(statistics) the mean value of the product of the deviations of two variates from their respective means
dampen	vt.	to make sth. less strong; restrain
document	vt.	to prove or support (sth.) with documents
motivate	vt.	to give an incentive for action
charter	vt.	to state officially that a new organization, town or university has been established and has special rights and privileges
depository	n.	a person or body receiving sth. in trust; a trustee; a storehouse

exposure	n.	the state of being in a place or situation where there is no protection from sth. harmful or unpleasant
accountability	n.	responsibility for one's decisions or actions
embed	vt.	to fix or set securely or deeply
engender	vt.	to make a feeling or situation exist

Comprehension
1. What does risk management refer to?
2. What are "risk identification" and "risk reduction"?
3. What is financial risk management?
4. Why is it necessary to find the correct place for risk management? And how?
5. What does an appropriate risk management system involve?

Translation
Please translate the parts in waves into Chinese.

Questions for Discussion
1. How do financial firms and non-financial firms address risk management?
2. Discuss the importance of risk management in banking.

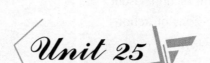

Passage

The Risk of Liberalization and Its Solution

The difficulty in assessing the risks of different financial instruments in different jurisdictions, and of the jurisdictions themselves, makes it almost impossible to calculate with confidence the risk-adjusted returns. This is notwithstanding gallant (and now much improved) monitoring efforts of the international financial institutions, such as the International Monetary Fund, and the valuable work of the commercial rating agencies. As a consequence, some jurisdictions get more, others get less, capital flows, in either direction, than justified, and financial markets overshoot. They can reach such an extent as to lead to systemic problems, when, for example, the weaker domestic financial institutions of emerging markets, hampered by their inability to identify and manage risks under the influence of globalization, collapse. Alternatively, domestic macroeconomic problems, considered to be benign on one day, all of a sudden become malignant the next, triggered possibly by some strange events; then sharp, destabilizing reversals of capital flow ensue, with debilitating consequences to the financial system and the economy.

All of this, of course, sounds familiar, with the Asian financial crisis of 1997 – 1998 still quite fresh in our minds. And so we all come to realize that for financial liberalization to produce the desired benefits it has to be accompanied by much greater discipline in pursuing prudent macroeconomic policies, and improved robustness in the financial system, including the financial infrastructure. This applies also to those jurisdictions wishing to maintain their current degree of openness, of their financial systems and markets, although it is also possible, and indeed individual jurisdictions have quite successfully chosen, to put up protective shields permanently or temporarily. "If you wish to play major league baseball, you'd better get used to the strong pitching," said a leading central banker in a post mortem of the Asian financial crisis—a telling description of the reality.

And the reality is often harsh, particularly for those who are less well endowed, for example, economies with financial markets that are small relative to the amount of international portfolio capital that could be mobilized by foreign investors but big enough to whet their appetite for profit. These relatively small financial markets may have to tolerate concentrated market positions and lack of transparency, in the hope of retaining foreign interests, but at the expense of increasing their vulnerability to the reversal of flows. Furthermore, the versatility of foreign funds and their higher sensitivity (than domestic funds) to shifts in market sentiment and policy changes, are such that, arguably, the market discipline imposed on macroeconomic policies of emerging markets may de facto be more stringent than those imposed on developed markets. Indeed, what is acknowledged by many as unsustainable, the large current account deficit in excess of 5% of GDP in the United States, has been sustained there for some time now, probably a lot longer than if it were run by an emerging market.

But there really is no magic formula or sequence for financial liberalization. For the sake of argument, in an economy with a domestic savings rate that is already high, where there is no shortage of funding for domestic investment, increasing the efficiency of domestic financial intermediation should arguably receive priority. Freeing up the capital account and allowing international mobility of portfolio capital would, of course, enable foreign savings to come in and would allow financial deepening. But it is important to be clear whether these are needed in the first place, whether the benefits justify the assumption of the associated risks and whether there is adequate risk management capability. In any case, the inflow of foreign savings under liberalization could well be more than compensated by the outflow domestic savings. Capital account liberalization, if the intention is to attract a net inflow of foreign savings, may therefore have to be structured and sequenced accordingly, involving, for a time, asymmetric international mobility of capital biased towards inflows. The fact that, in the financial liberalization of the Mainland, QFII has preceded QDII is a good example of this approach, although the threat of over-investment now strengthens very much the case for going ahead with QDII as quickly as possible.

In the final analysis, it has to be recognized that net capital inflow, whether in the form of direct investment or portfolio investment, under restricted or free circumstances, must by definition be mirrored by a deficit in the current account of the balance of payments. Long-term dependence on net capital inflow is unrealistic, just as it is unrealistic to sustain significant current account deficits indefinitely. This is not an argument against free and open financial markets. The efficiency gains in financial intermediation arising from foreign participation and competition should not be overlooked. The economic success of emerging markets in Asia, the financial crisis of 1997-1998 notwithstanding, would not have been possible if there had been financial repression instead of financial liberalization. The financial freedom of Hong Kong, furthermore, demonstrates this clearly. But beware of the risks.

Words & Expressions

jurisdiction	n.	the territorial range of authority or control
liberalization	n.	of finance, the removal by a government of controls over credit and interest rates, rates of exchange and the power of banks to lend and borrow money wherever they wish
financial instrument		an instrument having monetary value or recording a monetary transaction
rating agency		a company that rates the ability of a person or company to pay back a loan
overshoot	vi.	to shoot beyond or over (a target); aim too high
hamper	vt.	to prevent the free movement, action, or progress of
malignant	adj.	(of diseases) threatening to life
debilitating	adj.	impairing the strength and vitality
post mortem		discussion of an event after it has occurred
versatility	n.	having a wide variety of skills
de facto	adv.	(from Latin) in reality or fact; actually
stringent	adj.	demanding strict attention to rules and procedures
current account		that part of the balance of payments recording a nation's exports and imports of goods and services and transfer payments
capital account		(economics) that part of the balance of payments recording a nation's outflow and inflow of financial securities
QFII	(abbr.)	Qualified Foreign Institutional Investors
QDII	(abbr.)	Qualified Domestic Institutional Investors

Comprehension

1. What are the specific risks of financial liberalization mentioned in the text?
2. For financial liberalization to produce the desired benefits, what other accompanying policies should be adopted?
3. Why does the author say the reality is often harsh? What kind of reality does the author exhibit?
4. Does the author think that there is a magic formula for financial liberalization? How does he illustrate his opinion?
5. What attitude does the author hold toward financial liberalization, for or against?

Translation
Please translate the part in waves into Chinese.

Questions for Discussion
1. How does financial liberalization affect economic growth?
2. How well has financial liberalization worked for developing countries?

Passage

The Value of Being in Control
Luigi Zingales

Despite many differences throughout the world in the way companies are sold and acquired, there is one common element—investors care about control, which suggests it is valuable. But why? Luigi Zingales outlines why people will pay a lot to control a company.

This question of valuing control, though perhaps a little naive, is not without merit. By their very nature, all common shares have equal rights. A majority shareholder is not entitled to receive a penny more per share than all other shareholders. So why should any investor pay a premium to acquire control?

The only possible answer is that, although all shares are created equal, some are more equal than others.

What makes controlling shareholders more equal is that they have the right to shape corporate policy. The crucial question, then, becomes how this right translates into higher benefits for the controlling party that are not shared by other shareholders (the so-called "private benefits of control").

If private benefits of control exist, then it is easy to explain why control is valuable. But what exactly are they?

The academic literature often identifies them as the "psychic" value some shareholders attribute simply to being in control. For example, the Michelins probably would value being in control of the famous tyre company founded by their ancestors even if they were not to receive a penny from it.

Although this is certainly a factor in a number of cases, its practical importance is likely to be trivial.

A second, only slightly more convincing, explanation identifies the private benefits of control in the perquisites enjoyed by top executives (and not by their fellow shareholders who pay the tab). There is no lack of examples, as masterfully illustrated in the book *Barbarians at the Gate*. Many executives enjoy golfing and partying with world celebrities at their company's expense and using corporate jets to fly their friends and families around the country. Yet we have to admit that if this is what private benefits are all about we do not need to worry too much about the value of control. In the context of companies worth billions of dollars, the value of these perquisites is simply too small to matter.

Only in the presence of more significant sources of private benefits should the value of control play a prominent role in the theory and practice of finance.

Consider, for example, the value of the information a corporate executive acquires thanks to his or her role in the company. Some of this information pertains directly to the company's business. Some of it reflects potential opportunities in other more or less related areas.

It is fairly easy for a controlling shareholder to choose to exploit these opportunities through another company he or she owns or is associated with, with no advantage for the remaining shareholders. The net present value of these opportunities represents a private benefit of control.

Another source of private benefits is the possibility if internalizing, through other companies controlled by the same party, some of the externalities generated by corporate decisions.

Consider, for example, a shareholder who controls 51 percent of two companies, let's say A and B, operating in the same market. Suppose that there is excess capacity in this market and, thus, some plants need to be closed. In this situation the closure of any plant will reduce overcapacity and so will increase the value of all the other plants.

If the controlling shareholder closes some plants in company B, he or she will experience an increase in value not only of the B shares but also of the A shares. This increase in A shares is a benefit enjoyed by the controlling party and not by B's minority shareholders (unless they own the same quantity of A shares) and, thus, represents a private benefits of control.

A third source of private benefits is associated with the controlling party's ability to fix transfer prices between a company and its customers and suppliers.

A company controlled by its employees, for example, can pay higher wages and benefits to its workforce. Similarly, a bank controlled by one of its borrowers can make larger and cheaper loans to its parent company.

The ability to manipulate transfer prices can be used even in the absence of business dealings between the controlling company and its subsidiary. Imagine that company A owns 50 percent of company B and 100 percent of company C.

In that case A would find it profitable to transfer B's assets to C at a below-market price. For any dollar that B's assets are underestimated, company A loses 50 cents through its B holdings but gains one dollar through its C holdings. A net gain of 50 cents!

I am sure that at this point the reader is wondering whether most (if not all) of the sources of private benefits that I described are de facto illegal and, as such, more in the realm of interest of criminal investigators than financial economists.

In fact, there is no doubt that in their most extreme forms these strategies are illegal and extremely rare. Nevertheless, there are several reasons why we should expect more moderate versions of these strategies to be more pervasive.

First, in some countries some of these strategies are not illegal at all. Second, even when a law does exist it might be impossible to enforce. For example, educated economists can legitimately disagree on what is the "fair" transfer price of a certain asset or product. As a result, small deviations from the "fair" transfer price might be difficult or impossible to prove it in court. If these small deviations are applied to a large volume trade, however, they can easily generate sizeable private benefits. Finally, even if these distortions can be proved in court, it is possible that nobody has the incentive to do so. For example, it might be prohibitively expensive for small shareholders to sue management.

In other words, if private benefits of control were easily quantifiable, then those benefits would not be private (accruing only to the control group) any longer because outside shareholders would claim them in court.

Nevertheless, there are two indirect methods to try to assess empirically the magnitude of these private benefits of control.

The first method is very simple. Whenever a control block changes hands, they measure the difference between the price per share paid by the acquirer and the price quoted in the market the day after the announcement of the sale.

The market price represents an unbiased estimate of the value of a share for minority shareholders. Any amount paid in excess of it by the acquirer of the control block represents a minimum estimate of the buyer's willingness to pay for the private benefits of control he or she expects to enjoy.

Using a sample of control block transfers in the US, they find that the value of control is approximately 4 percent of the total market value of a company.

This method also makes clear why the takeover premium cannot be used by itself as a measure of the private benefits of control. When a takeover is announced, the market price incorporates two pieces of information:(1) that the company is likely to be run by a different management team; (2) that somebody is willing to pay a premium for control.

The takeover premium is a combination of these two elements and, in general, it is impossible to separate them. Only when there are two classes of common stock with differential voting rights can we try to disentangle these two components.

This leads to the second method of estimating the value of private benefits of control.

By using the price difference between two classes of stock, with similar or identical dividend rights but different voting rights, one can easily obtain an estimate of the value of a vote. If control is valuable, then corporate votes, which allocate control, should be valuable as well. How valuable?

It depends on how decisive some votes are in allocating control and how valuable control is. If one can find a reasonable proxy for the strategic value of votes in winning control—for example in forming a winning coalition block—then one can infer the value of control from the relationship between the market price of the votes and their strategic role.

I have inferred the value of control from the relationship between the value of corporate votes and a synthetic measure of the distribution of voting power called the Shapley value.

Interestingly, when I applied this method to a sample of US companies I obtained the same value as Barclay and Holderness (4 percent). By contrast, when I applied it to a sample of Italian companies I estimated the value of control at 30 percent of the market value of equity.

In spite of the magnitude of this estimate, all the evidence I collected indicates that, if anything, it underestimates the true value of control in Italy. But why should the value of control be so much higher in Italy than in the US? And what should we expect it to be in other countries?

Since the value of control is simply the present value of the private benefits enjoyed by the controlling party, the answer is easy.

The magnitude of the private benefits of control, and thus the value of control, depends on the degree of protection offered to minority investors in each country. Without proper disclosure, large investors can more easily hide their abuses and hence find it easier to take advantage of their controlling position.

Similarly, lax law enforcement makes it more difficult to detect and punish these abuses, making them more attractive.

That small investors are better protected in the US than in Continental Europe is not only consistent with casual empiricism but has been documented in a systematic way by La Porta et al.

But even in the US, privately held companies carry large control premiums (minority discounts). Interestingly, the reason appraisers adduce for this premium is the lack of protection of minority shareholders in privately held business.

So it is not the good nature of Americans that restrains them from abusing their control position, but rather the rigid oversight by the Securities and Exchange Commission. It is not unusual, for example, for the SEC to investigate large personal expenses that a controlling shareholder bills to his or her company.

Interestingly, once we admit the existence of sizeable private benefits of control, a lot of the standard finance results break down.

For example, the value of a company cannot any longer be estimated simply by multiplying the market price of a share but by the number of shares. If one shareholder controls a majority of votes, the market price will simply reflect the value of minority shares and will grossly underestimate the value of a company.

By contrast, when two large shareholders are fighting to reach a majority, the market price of a stock will be mainly influenced by the control value and will overestimate the total value of a company.

More importantly, the efficient working of the financial market may be jeopardized. Large controlling shareholders will be more interested in maximizing the value of their private benefits than the total market value of their company.

Consequently, investors, anticipating this behaviour, will shy away from buying the stocks. This, in turn, will lead to an underdevelopment of security markets. The paucity of observations notwithstanding, there would appear to be a strong negative correlation between the magnitude of the voting premium and the size of the stock market relative to the gross domestic product. This is an important lesson developing countries should not ignore.

Words & Expressions

perquisite	n.	a payment or profit received in addition to a regular wage or salary, especially a benefit expected as one's due
tab	n.	a bill or check, such as one for a meal in a restaurant
pertain	vi.	to have to do with or be relevant to
manipulate	vt.	to influence or manage shrewdly or deviously
deviation	n.	the act of moving away from what is normal or acceptable; a difference from what is expected or acceptable
accrue	vi.	to come as a natural increase or advantage, esp. financial; accumulate
disentangle	vt.	to separate different ideas, arguments, etc. that have become confused
proxy	n.	authority to represent sb. else (esp. in voting at an election)
adduce	vt.	to put (sth.) forward as an example or as proof
jeopardize	vt.	to pose a threat to; present a danger to; put at risk
paucity	n.	smallness of number or quantity

Comprehension

1. What does "private benefits of control" refer to?
2. How many sources of private benefits are mentioned in the text? What specifically are they?
3. Why can't the takeover premium be used by itself as a measure of the private benefits of control?
4. Can we use the methods put forward in the text to assess the magnitude of the private benefits of control in a specific company? And how?
5. What consequences will the existence of sizable private benefits of control lead to?

Translation
Please translate the parts in waves into Chinese.

Questions for Discussion
1. If sizable private benefits of control exist in a company, should small shareholders sue the management?
2. Are there any policies that the government can adopt to protect small investors?

Unit 27

Passage

Work beyond 2010
Richard Scase

Richard Scase highlights the changes that will increasingly affect the way businesses operate.

In the past, companies functioned as internally integrated systems: creating structures, functions, and tasks as they grew that managed all of their activities "in-house". This enabled the directors to keep a tight control over these various activities and was most often undertaken by applying the principles of hierarchical line management. Managers gave orders and workers dutifully executed them. A culture of compliance predominated and the organization, with the aim of functioning like a well-oiled machine, operated by reference to precisely stipulated job descriptions.

The management of information is a good case in point. In the past this was a straightforward corporate activity. It was conducted by tiers of line managers whose responsibilities were to ensure that information was managed on a "need to know" basis. The structuring of this information was hierarchical and reflected the needs of the organization rather than customer requirements. Structured on the basis of specialist departments—sales, marketing, accounts, and so on—companies were highly fragmented in their internal and external operational practices.

This meant that the management of information was highly focused and localized. It could rarely be integrated across the organization to develop customer-driven innovative products and services. It was also difficult for companies to focus on their core corporate competencies and leverage them for competitive success. If there were any centralized corporate handling of data it was of a non-strategic kind—for example, customer accounts, staff payrolls, and so on. This explains the old-fashioned popularity of computer mainframes. Different departments stored data on them that was used for their own specialist purposes; it was not a shared resource.

This paradigm is well-known and large numbers of businesses still try to function in this way. However, it neglects organization's hidden inefficiencies. The growing recognition of these inefficiencies is bringing about a core rethink of how businesses should operate and, with this, a reappraisal of the role of management. The outcome is the emergence of new organizational forms that will have repercussions for the future nature of work and employee skills.

Intellectual Capital and Innovation

Traditional forms of organization are becoming redundant because the future business will not be a manufacturing enterprise. By the year 2010, only 10 percent of the labor force in the UK will be engaged in manufacturing.

The twenty-first century will witness the continuing growth of the information economy, with businesses trading on the basis of the various value-added services that they can provide. This means their key asset is intellectual capital and not, as in the past, machinery and the capacity to produce standardized products for either high-volume or niche markets (as is the case for large numbers of small and medium-sized enterprises).

Intellectual capital is the knowledge a company possesses to be innovative in continuously developing new products or services that are relevant for gaining competitive advantage in its targeted markets. In other words, in an information economy, IT is the basis for a company's core competencies. Everything else that may have been undertaken within traditional, highly integrated enterprises can now be outsourced, often on a global basis. The key challenge for businesses is to nurture creativity and innovation. It is the ability to do this that will differentiate successful, high-performing and competitive businesses from the rest.

How can creativity be nurtured so there is continuous innovation? Many lessons can be learned from the ways in which many small and medium-sized enterprises operate. Those that are high-performing have a clear vision. The founding owners have a strong idea of where they want their businesses to—and, importantly, so do their employees. There is an employer-employee partnership in which the vision is shared. The principle may be simple, but its implementation requires the presence of a range of organizational features.

- There is open, honest, and fluid communication around all matters that are likely to affect the company's future.
- This, in turn, demands the existence of a culture of high trust between employers and employees.
- This in itself requires that employees are trained and given the capacity to develop their own talents for their self-development as well as for the good of the enterprise. They must feel that they are stakeholders, participating in the rewards of the company as it grows. This can be in a variety of forms, ranging from equity stakes (as in many business partnerships) to profit sharing and career prospects.

It is within such organizational contexts that creativity is nurtured. These features account for the rapid growth of many small and medium-sized firms in such diverse industries as high technology, bioscience, professional services, advertising, and entertainment. Often the organization attributes are nurtured around the "charisma" or the personalities of the founder-owner. Although this can be an advantage, it is not an absolute necessity. What is vital for high performance is continuous innovation through leveraging the creativity of employees through the organizational processes mentioned above.

Product innovation through employee creativity requires the psychological contract between employer and employee to be redefined. There must be a shift from compliance to internalized commitment.

Essentially, this means that employees are excited by their jobs—they eat, sleep, and drink their work. Their jobs are at the heart of their personal identities and inherent to their notions of self. Again, it is only through managing the business as a partnership between employer and employees that this can be achieved.

The Physical Workplace

If, in the past, the workplace was where work was done, in the information economy it is where ideas are exchanged and problems solved. This normally requires close working relationships among colleagues and the cultivation of positive team dynamics. It not only puts a premium on selecting employees who are technically competent, but also on recruiting people who are personally compatible with others in the business. The architecture and design of the workplace need to facilitate communication and teamwork.

Through the strategic use of information networks, companies can now operate as highly decentralized yet tightly integrated operating units spread across the globe. At the same time, and on a global basis, they can develop and pursue their business strategies through supply chain partnerships and strategic alliances.

This capability gives companies flexibility in their business practices. These are not steady-state organizations. On the contrary, they have mobility in both their internal and external operations. This continual change is driven by the need for continuous innovation. The outcome is the ever-transforming corporation that is forever redesigning its internal processes and its external trading linkages. If organizations of the past were characterized by stability, those of the future have the paradigm of constant change.

What is striking about businesses that compete on the basis of their intellectual capital is how they convey the physical impression that nothing much is being produced. This is because the workplace is designed to encourage face-to-face encounters among colleagues for solving problems and generating new ideas. A high proportion of floor space is designed as "public areas", consisting of comfortable sofas arranged around vending machines. These areas are the nerve centers of creative businesses. Through discussion in these areas, colleagues develop ideas and then turn to their "private spheres" (and this is increasingly at home instead of at the workplace) to explore further the potential and feasibility. These thoughts will then be fed back to colleagues in the coffee area on a later occasion.

It will become taken for granted that staff should not have their own desks or exclusive use of office space. Hot-desking will be commonplace. People will spend less time working in offices. It may be necessary for them to attend corporate premises for meetings with colleagues but, increasingly, more time will be spent working on projects at home and away from the office with customers and business partners.

In the US roughly 24 percent of the labor force is mobile. In the UK the figure is 35 percent and growing. By 2010 it will reach over 60 percent—a staggering change in the patterns and culture of work. This will reduce the need for large corporate buildings, which will contribute to a sharp reduction in overhead costs—a hidden but substantial contribution that network systems can make to business profitability.

The process of innovation is not formally structured. It is not a specialist or compartmentalized activity, as is often the case in traditional manufacturing companies. Instead, it is located at the very heart of the business process. Employers cannot tell employees to be creative—intellectual capital does not work in this way. What employers can do is to provide the organizational and architectural contexts that facilitate employees' creativity, and then reward employees so they have a shareholder's interest in the outcomes of innovation. This often means more than simply material rewards. It can be part ownership of patents, as in bioscience, or the opportunity for professional recognition, as in the entertainment industry.

Location is also an important factor for leveraging creativity and fully utilizing the intellectual capital of a business. Why is it that the center for the global entertainment industry continues to be in congested Los Angeles? Why do advertising agencies locate in parts of London and software companies in the UK's Thames Valley? It is because these geographic areas constitute clusters of tacit knowledge, of intellectual skills from which all firms benefit. Pools of talents become geographically concentrated and then shape the character of local infrastructures. Therefore, the local labor markets from which these companies recruit consist of pools of appropriate intellectual capital. In many ways these are similar to the industrial districts of the early Industrial Revolution, where cultures became established that enhanced the capabilities of each of the separate businesses.

The Limits of the Virtual Workplace

There are limits to the extent to which information technology can completely abolish the need for the workplace. A barrier to the adoption of the virtual organization, enabled by information technology, is the need for those with intellectual capital to interface in spontaneous and unstructured ways to leverage creativity to develop innovative products and services. In order for companies to be competitive in the information economy, they need to redesign their operational processes, management styles and cultures. This will require self-confident leadership in which openness and informality are encouraged. The design and architecture of their workplaces will need to embody these assumptions. Businesses will have to function as partnerships of all their aspects, from strategic decision making to the structuring of reward system.

Without these mechanisms in place, intellectual capital—as the core asset of the information-based business—will simply walk out of the door. Unlike machinery in factories, people—especially those with creative knowledge—cannot be bolted to the floor.

Words & Expressions

compliance	n.	the practice of obeying rules or requests made by people in authority
payroll	n.	a list of people employed by a company showing the amount of money to be paid to each of them
charisma	n.	the powerful personal quality that some people have to attract and impress other people
compatible	adj.	(of people, ideas, arguments, principles, etc.) suited; that can exist together
staggering	adj.	astonishing, shocking
overhead	adj.	connected with the general costs of running a business or an organization, for example, paying for rent or electricity
tacit	adj.	that is suggested indirectly or understood, rather than said in words
interface	vi.	to interact; communicate with sb., especially in a work-related situation
bolt	vt.	to fasten (together) with bolts; make fast

Comprehension

1. What is the traditional way of the management of information? Is there any problem with it?
2. How do you understand intellectual capital?
3. What organizational contexts can nurture creativity? How will employer-employee partnership evolve in the future?
4. Is the traditional workplace necessary in the information economy? And why?
5. What is the process of innovation?
6. What are the limits of the virtual workplace?

Translation
Please translate the parts in waves into Chinese.

Questions for Discussion
1. In your opinion, what should be the appropriate relationship between employer and employee?
2. What kind of workplace do you prefer, traditional or virtual?

Unit 28

Passage

What's Hot on the Cyberspace Hit List

Electronic commerce is a major part of every industry and marketplace these days. So-called e-business such as Amazon.com, America Online and eBay are all less than 10 years old but have already become household names and major players in the transformation of the United States into an information-based economy. Faced with this rapid and dynamic change, staid older businesses that want to remain vital and effective have found it necessary to refocus their own operations to encompass the Internet and electronic commerce. Some, such as IBM and Disney, have made successful transitions while others have faltered.

The music industry is an especially interesting arena for e-commerce competition—one in which both newcomers and established firms continue to struggle to find just the right approach to integrating the Internet into their operations. Giants like Universal Music Group <www.universalmusic.com>, Warner Music Group <www.timewarner.com/corp/about/music/index.html>, Sony Music <www.sonymusic.com>, BMG entertainment <www.bmgentertainment.com>, and EMI <www.emi.com> have long dominated the recorded-music business. However, they are facing new and complex challenges as the Internet plays an increasingly significant role in their marketplace. New e-businesses pose both serious threats and significant opportunities for these media giants.

Consider the case of David Goldberg and Launch Media. When Goldberg, a music fanatic, was only 24 years old, he landed a plum job as director of new business development for Capitol Records. Goldberg was interested in extending the Capitol library of popular music, which ranged from Frank Sinatra to the Beatles, into new arenas. He wanted to promote Capitol's music products on CD-ROM games and to focus heavily on new and emerging forms of electronic media for promoting and delivering music to consumers.

But senior executives at Capitol weren't interested. They listened politely, but they adopted few of his ideas and gave him little encouragement in his efforts to push into new products and product lines. They apparently believed that the old tried-and-true method of recording music on disks and tapes, advertising and promoting new recordings in magazines and on the radio, and then distributing them through traditional retailing channels was never going to change.

Finally, Goldberg left Capitol in frustration and created Launch Media <www.launchmedia.com>, which has quickly become one of the top five music-information sites on the Internet. NBC and Sony Music are two of the biggest investors in Goldberg's fledgling enterprise, and when the firm went public in April 1999, the value of his personal stake mushroomed to $12 million. But unlike some entrepreneurs in other industries and markets, Goldberg has never been interested in taking over the music business. What he wants to do is to change it. And more and more industry experts are coming around to his point of view. "Our role," says one industry consultant who sees things in Goldberg's way, "is to teach the industry to do things differently."

Some industry experts worried that Internet sites would render traditional recording companies obsolete—that consumers would simply download all the music they wanted directly from various Web sites controlled by artists or upstart Web outfits and that the recording companies would be squeezed out. But those in the know quickly realized that this isn't how things would work out. Instead, the Internet is emerging as a new catalyst for old and new music businesses alike. Web sites like launch.com are becoming platforms for more and more interaction among consumers, performers, and recording labels. As you can see in Table 1, the five largest music-information sites on the Internet are attracting millions of visitors each month—and generating millions of dollars in revenues.

Table 1 Plugging into Cyberspace

	Visitors in August	Revenues[1]
MTV.COM	2.2 million	$9.9 million
MP3.COM	2.0 million	$2.6 million
TUNES.COM	1.2 million	$1.4 million
UBL.COM	1.2 million	$3.7 million
LAUNCH.COM	1.1 million	$4.7 million

[1] First-half 1999, from all websites in the corporate family, not just the site listed.

The big companies still play a vital role in all this information-related activity. For example, they still control most of the recordings, handle much of the advertising and promotion, and provide the "human contact" that remains an essential part of all entertainment enterprises. Consumers, meanwhile, can visit websites in the comfort of their own homes and download trial music cuts to sample music that they might want to buy. Then they can easily purchase CDs—in addition to concert tickets, posters, shirts, and other paraphernalia—directly from the same sites. Granted, performers can leverage bigger cuts of the profits, but Goldberg and others like to point out the obvious advantages of keeping everybody happy.

The challenge of building and sustaining a new business to meet changing and newly emerging customer needs is as common to small firms like Launch Media as it is to billion-dollar corporations such as Warner Music Group or Sony Music. A changing marketplace creates a need for the kind of innovative responses that have long characterized business in the United States. Such responses require vision, careful attention to quality and customer service, substantial financial commitment, internal accounting controls, and well-defined marketing strategies designed to help businesses grow over time.

These and a host of other forces provide the main themes for stories of success and failure that are told repeatedly in the annals of enterprise in the United States. These forces are also the key factors in the US market economy. You will see, too, that although the world's economic systems differ markedly, standards for evaluating success or failure are linked to a system's capacity to achieve certain basic goals.

Words & Expressions

staid	adj.	settled in character and conduct; sober
encompass	vt.	to include in scope; include as part of something broader; have as one's sphere or territory
integrate	vt.	to make into a whole; combine into a whole
product line		a particular kind of way to produce product or merchandise
tried-and-true	adj.	tested and proved to be reliable
retailing channel		a way of selling a company's product directly to consumers
fledgling	adj.	young and inexperienced
go public		to change from being a private to a public limited company
stake	n.	a right or legal share of something; a financial involvement with something
render	vt.	to cause to become
obsolete	adj.	old; no longer in use or valid or fashionable
upstart	adj.	newly born, emerging
catalyst	n.	something that causes an important event to happen
generate	vt.	to produce
paraphernalia	n.	equipment consisting of miscellaneous articles needed for a particular operation or sport

leverage	vt.	to influence
annals	n.	reports of the work of a society or learned body; a chronological account of events in successive years

Comprehension

1. Why do staid older businesses need to make transitions? And how to make transitions?
2. Do you think giants in the music industry are facing new and complex challenges? And why?
3. What have you got from the case of David Goldberg?
4. What does Table 1 "Plugging into Cyberspace" illustrate?
5. What does a changing marketplace calls for?

Translation

Please translate the part in waves into Chinese.

Questions for Discussion

1. How much do you know about cyberspace?
2. Talk about the advantages and disadvantages of e-business.

Unit 29

Passage

To Be a Well-off Witkey?
Li Qian

A "witkey" is a person who sells knowledge and experience to others via the Internet. What are the opportunities and challenges of this new and rapidly expanding area of e-commerce?

It was one o'clock in the morning, and Huang Weiguo was hunched over his keyboard, busily applying the finishing touches to the product he was about to send to his client via a witkey website. He had spent two similarly tedious late nights staring at his screen, making sure that the package he returned would be a high-quality job. "It's a very demanding job, but the hours can be flexible. What's more, you can find the work you specialize in directly on these witkey websites."

The 23-year-old is an art and design major at the Shanxi University of Science and Technology. For the past two years, he has been easing the financial burdens of his studies by working as a witkey. Huang Weiguo recalls his first experience, "In early 2005, my friend put me on to a witkey website. Out of curiosity, I took on a job to design a software poster. The client liked it, and paid me 150 yuan."

Huang was immediately hooked. In spite of various setbacks or rejections over the past two years, Huang Weiguo managed to rake in a total of RMB 20,000. That's a decent sum of cash in the witkey world—it's a buyer's market.

Now in his third year of university, and with graduation on the horizon, Huang Weiguo is looking forward to his first real job. His experience as a witkey will, Huang reckons, bring him more options. He explains, "Being a witkey gives me the chance to get real work experience, and increases my professional competence. All this experience will be useful when I go up against others in the job hunt."

Cyber Revolution

Log onto www.k68.cn, and you'll find a wealth of opportunities for those with witkey talent. Most require specialized skills, but some do not. For instance, you can make RMB

200 to help a couple come up with a name for their new-born daughter, solving a flash-making problem will earn you RMB 50, and you can pick up RMB 1,000 for helping a company to design a logo.

Would-be clients post their requirements—and the price they're willing to pay—on the witkey websites. Witkeys browse the site, select the tasks they're interested in, and contact the potential clients. The successful applicant takes 80 percent of the payment, with 20 percent going to the website host.

"The evolution of witkey is actually a revolution," says Kang Lufa, boss of K68. "Gifted youths stand to earn 10,000 yuan a month working in Beijing's advertising agencies, but their counterparts in smaller cities and towns might earn only a tenth of that. Our website helps in part to close that gap. What's more, the service also helps small and medium-sized companies that cannot afford the high fees of professional design firms. On our website, they can set the price to suit their budgets. Even if they can afford just 100 yuan, someone out there will be willing to take on the project for that fee."

In fact, witkey websites are closely related to blogs in that they both stem from BBS. While blogs or web forums work on an "ask-answer" basis, witkey sites work on a "request-offer service" mode. The value of knowledge is embodied in the process. And with its uncomplicated payment transfer system, witkey not only establishes a platform for the trade of intellectual services, but also helps to facilitate the expansion of e-commerce.

A New Vocation

Though still in their infancy, witkey websites are experiencing something of a growth spurt. According to the Research Report on China's Witkey Business Model and Investment Prospects, more than 40 witkey websites—with 600,000 users—have come into existence in the past two years. It predicts the number of witkey users will rocket to 9 million by the end of the year. The report should please witkey website operators. At the moment, their revenues are paltry—K68 pulls in about RMB 30,000 per month from its 130,000 registered members.

These days, most witkeys are designers, consultants, copywriters, and undergraduates, and their average age is 25. Many dream of forging a career as a witkey, so they can be their own boss, at their own office, in their own home.

But Kang Lufa says this will take time. "Witkey is a brand-new business pattern, and competition is fierce. In fact, just three percent of registered witkeys actually earn money, and even the outstanding talents rarely make more than 10,000 yuan a year!" Since clients set the fees, they usually offer a fraction of the market price. So there's no point in giving up the day job just yet.

The witkey world has other drawbacks, too. The nature of the system requires all work to be posted online before a penny is paid, so that clients can choose the piece they like best. This leads to two problems. First, other witkeys can steal and modify a particularly good application, and make sure they get the job. Second, the clients themselves can log in as a new user, steal a design they fancy and "sell" it to themselves—free of charge.

Meanwhile, a lack of supervision and control also poses problems. As long as one knows how to register on a website, one can issue any assignment, like one's university thesis, or immoral or illegal assignments. The hows and the whos of supervision and control urgently need to be addressed.

Words & Expressions

hunch	vt.	to arch one's back
ease	vt.	to make easier; alleviate
rake in		to earn as income (a lot of money)
go up against		compete with
counterpart	n.	a person or thing having the same function or characteristics as another
facilitate	vt.	to make easy or easier; help
paltry	adj.	contemptibly small in amount
forge	vt.	to make something, usually for a specific function
pose	vt.	to be the cause of (something difficult to deal with)

Comprehension

1. What does a witkey refer to? And what do you think of it?
2. Why is the witkey world referred to as a buyer's market?
3. Describe the way that witkey websites work.
4. How do you understand "The evolution of witkey is actually a revolution"?
5. Why does Kang Lufa say that "There's no point in giving up the day job just yet"?
6. What are the drawbacks of the witkey world?

Translation

Please translate the parts in waves into Chinese.

Questions for Discussion

1. Say what you know about blogs and BBS.
2. Can you put forward some practical and workable suggestions to help witkey websites operate legally and properly?

Unit 30

Passage

Virtual World, Real Fortune
Liu Yunyun

Online gaming is finding ways to make a profit, and China is cashing in.

To those few businessmen relatively unplugged from the era of the Internet, online gaming should still start to mean something. When it comes to sales revenue of over 6.54 billion yuan in a year with an estimated 30 percent annual increase, the unreal should become real for even the most old-school of profit seekers.

According to the 2006 Gaming Industry Report jointly prepared by the China Game Publication Association and International Data Corp., the online gaming market of China reached 6.54 billion yuan last year, up 73.5 percent compared with 2005. Surprisingly, this industry took in a mere 310 million yuan just five years ago.

Kou Xiaowei, Deputy Director of General Administration of Press and Publication (GAPP) in charge of online publication, stated in early January that the "gaming industry has become one of the creative industries with the most development potential." Kou added that the Chinese online gaming industry has been recognized by the world as the biggest emerging market.

The above-mentioned report also shows that in 2006, over 31.12 million Chinese played online games.

Market Driven

Backed by the world's largest population, the number of China's online game players is bound to increase every year. Both domestic and foreign game developers and operators are seeking shares of this ballooning market.

But one question remains: how can operators make money from a virtual world? In the past, players had to buy certain cards to get access to an online game. However, currently, most of the operators don't charge players due to the cut-throat market competition. To find profits, the game operators turn to selling virtual gear, including clothing and special weapons, to players to enhance their gaming experience. That virtual gear costs real money and satisfies "human beings' inner desire to be powerful and dominant in one world," said Zhang Yang, a 25-year-old online gamer.

Zhang added that every one of his classmates in university played online games and those who didn't were laughed at.

"It's trendy," said Zhang.

NetEase.com, Shanda Entertainment, 9you.com, Kingsoft Corp. and Tencent Inc. are the major market players in the online gaming field. Most of them create their own games and also import online games from foreign countries. In 2006, NetEase replaced Shanda as the market leader.

According to CTR Market Research, about 68 percent of netizens play online games and the average age of online game players is 24. Those people will spend an average 188 yuan each month.

Domestic vs. Imported

Attracted by the lucrative market, online gaming giants have flowed into the Chinese market, such as Blizzard Entertainment, whose *World of Warcraft* amazes Chinese online game players.

However, as the examination and approval procedures for imported online games are stricter than domestic ones, many overseas online gaming companies would rather set up joint venture companies with local Chinese ones.

Earlier, many Chinese online game operators heavily depended on foreign game developers who were in a dominant position in the industrial chain. For instance, Shanda Entertainment, established in 1999, is one of China's first online game operators. It once focused on providing services for South Korean online games such as *Legend of Mir*, *Fortress 2* and *Shattered Galaxy*. The service charge and revenue brought about by selling virtual gear made Shanda's owner Chen Tianqiao a legend worth 6 billion yuan and ranked the second richest IT mogul according to the 2006 China IT Rich List released by Rupert Hoogeverf.

"Owing to the lack of indigenous Chinese games, many game products coming from different cultures and value systems had an adverse impact on Chinese youngsters. This forced Chinese game operators to develop their own games," said Wang Hui, Deputy General Manager of JoyChina, an online gaming company.

Therefore, Chinese companies took up the challenge to develop online games and to market them to the game players. At present, domestic Chinese games take up about 64 percent of the total online gaming market in China.

In the meantime, Chinese online games are also exported to foreign countries.

"Chinese online games are popular among foreign players," said Ren Jian, CEO of Kingsoft Corp. "The rich culture and history provide enormous resources for online game development."

It is estimated that China had sales revenue of over $20 million in the overseas market in 2006, mostly to neighboring countries like Viet Nam and Japan.

However, as the 25-year-old online game player Zhang said, "Domestic online games are too simple and don't challenge much."

Foreign online gaming companies are superior in capital supply and have powerful research and development. When China further loosens its restriction on those companies, domestic online gaming companies will suffer.

Currently, according to the 2006 Gaming Industry Report, foreign online games account for about a 40 percent market share in China.

"Among us players, we tend to believe if it is produced by the US Blizzard, it must be good," said Zhang.

One thing is noticeable. The popularity of online gaming does not always mean a profit, especially for domestically-made games.

The 2006 Gaming Industry Report shows that only 10 – 15 percent of domestic game producers and operators are profitable now while most of the companies can only make ends meet or are even on the brink of bankruptcy.

Delving into the Future Market

The 2006 Gaming Industry Report estimates the sales revenue of the online gaming publication industry will reach 24.43 billion yuan with an annual growth of 30.2 percent.

With the prevalence of the Internet, the online gaming industry will expand beyond the large and medium-sized cities. Shi Yuzhu, President of Zhengtu Game, pointed out that according to their investigation statistics, online gaming in three big Chinese cities including Beijing, Shanghai and Guangzhou only takes up 3 percent of the whole online gaming industry. Shi suggested counties and rural areas would become the major arenas for large online gaming operators.

Kou of GAPP pointed out three kinds of games or gaming services which would probably become more profitable in 2007.

The first is a combination of advertisement and online games. Currently, online games usually make a profit by selling gear and weapons or other derivative publications. But the operational mode has been broken up. In 2006, Volkswagen marketed its new Polo car through entering cooperation with a popular online game called *Race Fever* developed by Shanda Entertainment. In the same year, Coca-Cola advertised its products by joining hands with a hot online game called *Backyard Basketball*.

Kou said the second growth point for the industry is sport games as the Beijing 2008 Olympics approaches. The most popular games in 2006 were related to sports in one way or another, like *Backyard Basketball* and *Crazy Racing*. Kou pointed out that online sports games vividly mimic all kinds of real sports and become popular among players. One of the other major reasons is that sports games are viewed favorably by the Chinese Government. Kou stated that in 2007, the Chinese Government would loosen restriction on such games and encourage their development.

The cell phone gaming market is also significant. The 2006 Gaming Industry Report shows cell phone gaming has a market of 1.48 billion yuan, up 50.2 percent compared with the previous year. Kou said with the advent of the 3G era, cell phone online gaming would take off to even higher levels.

Words & Expressions

online game		games played using the Internet
ballooning market		a market that is becoming inflated
cutthroat	*adj.*	ruthless; intense
virtual gear		equipment, clothing, etc. produced to make users feel as if they are in real space
netizen	*n.*	net citizen
joint venture		an agreement between two companies to work together on a particular job, usually in order to share any risk involved
mogul	*n.*	a very rich, important or influential person
capital supply		wealth or property that may be used to produce more wealth
bankruptcy	*n.*	a situation in which a person or business becomes bankrupt
delve	*vi.*	to try to find information about sth.; study sth.
derivative	*adj.*	derived from sth. else; not original

Comprehension

1. What is reported on Chinese online gaming industry?
2. How can operators make a profit from online gaming in the past and at present?
3. Please give a general introduction to the development of Chinese online gaming.
4. What is the condition of domestic game producers and operators?
5. What are the three kinds of games or gaming services which would probably become more profitable in 2007 according to Kou Xiaowei?

Translation

Please translate the part in waves into Chinese.

Questions for Discussion

1. What do you think are the real purposes of online gaming producers and operators?
2. Do you think online gaming is necessary? And in your opinion, what is the point of online gaming?

Passage

Hanging by a Thread
Jim Erickson

An Asia-wide communications blackout raises questions about how to bolster the Internet.

The Global Telecommunications industry passed a little-noticed milestone last month when the US Federal Communications Commission (FCC) announced it was dropping a long-standing requirement that holders of amateur radio licenses be proficient in Morse code. These days, few save hobbyists use electronic dots and dashes for messaging. But in 1858, when the first undersea communications cable linking two continents was strung between the US and the UK, Morse code was the industry standard. A century and a half later, the FCC's move makes it an all-but-dead language.

Primitive though Morse may be, the world may want to keep it alive, if only as a backup when global communications networks crash—as they did spectacularly on Dec. 26 when an earthquake off China's Taiwan's coast damaged seven undersea fiber-optic cables that handle some 90% of phone calls and data traffic in the region. Millions of homes and businesses across Asia were left without the Internet access, e-mail and international phone connections. Financial markets were interrupted. And those lucky enough to connect to overseas websites experienced exasperatingly sluggish data-transfer speeds. While most services have been at least partially restored, a flotilla of repair vessels is expected to be working on the knocked-out cables for up to four weeks before networks are back to normal.

Communications blackouts aren't uncommon—in 2005, for example, Pakistan was cut off from the Internet for 12 days after a fishing boat accidentally snagged its main international connection; sharks have even been blamed for biting into lightly armored lines. But outages on the scale of this Asia-wide meltdown aren't supposed to happen. And with the march of globalization, companies are more dependent than ever on global networks, which makes the threat of communications paralysis particularly unsettling. So what can be done to prevent future blackouts?

The answer: not much—at least not immediately. In theory, the global Internet is highly resistant to catastrophic failure because it's a mesh of interconnected smaller networks, all providing alternative data pathways should any single link fail. Indeed, Asia's abundant data capacity and plentiful circuits—a legacy of rampant overbuilding of undersea cable during the tech boom—ensured that most traffic was quickly rerouted after the quake, restoring crucial services such as phone connections. Some of the overflow was also handled by satellite systems, which are normally too costly and lack the bandwidth of terrestrial networks.

But the Internet as it exists today is far from shockproof. It has been built by independent consortia of private telecom companies and investors, and network design has been driven by economics. Reliability is important, of course, but intercontinental cable systems can cost billions of dollars, so they tend to connect to countries where demand is greatest and they often lack costly parallel backup circuits that would be underused most of the time. Vulnerabilities exist, and the recent quake found a chink in the armor. It struck in the Luzon Strait south of Taiwan, an area that has an unusual concentration of major undersea cables. "It's quite an exceptional event to have so many cables tear at once," says Gary Chan, a computer-engineering professor at the Hong Kong University of Science and Technology. But China's Taiwan is a major commercial center situated between South and North Asia, so dozens of the links run to or near the island.

While the cables are at least 20 km apart, the magnitude 6.7 quake was powerful enough to shake or rupture a 300-km-long area of seabed. Given this temblor's force, says Ha Yung-Kuen, acting director-general of Hong Kong's office of the Telecommunications Authority (OFTA), "You can imagine the damage it would make to submarine cables. Maybe mountains become valleys, and valleys become mountains."

This month, says Ha, organizations like OFTA will hold discussions with telecom companies about faster rerouting procedures in the event of future cable failures. But it's up to the companies that own and lease the networks to iron out emergency procedures, which are complicated by contractual obligations and pricing agreements. The best solution, says Chan, is the construction of more pathways. China's Internet population alone increased by 30% last year; at current growth rates, China is projected to reach maximum capacity on its current networks by 2008. More cable networks are in the works. One consortium plans to invest $500 million to lay the first transpacific cable directly linking China and the US, while another is planning a link between Southeast Asia and the US, bypassing Taiwan of China. Technology is also being developed for "smart" networks that could automatically allocate bandwidth where needed, making disaster recovery faster—but all operators would need to adopt it.

In the meantime, it's impossible to rule out more catastrophic network failures. Better keep that Morse code guide handy.

Words & Expressions

blackout	n.	a suspension of radio, TV broadcasting or network
save	prep.	except
backup	n.	extra help or support that you can get if necessary
flotilla	n.	a group of boats or small ships sailing together
meltdown	n.	a disaster comparable to a nuclear meltdown
chink	n.	a narrow opening in sth.
rupture	vt.	to make sth. such as a container or a pipe break or burst; be broken or burst
temblor	n.	[AmE] earthquake
iron out		to get rid of any problems or difficulties that are affecting sth.
rule out		to prevent sb. from doing sth; to prevent sth. from happening

Comprehension

1. What did the earthquake off China's Taiwan's coast cause on Dec. 26?
2. From the passage, what is communications blackout?
3. Why is the Internet today far from shockproof?
4. What does China do while facing the increasing Internet population?
5. What is the author's suggestion? And why?

Translation

Please translate the parts in waves into Chinese.

Questions for Discussion

1. Do you think Morse code should be kept or not? Why?
2. Expound your views on the importance of the Internet. How can we bolster it?

Passage

Spam, to Go

Kathleen Kingsbury

Advertisers are homing in on mobile phones as the next great marketing medium.

Perhaps it was too good to last. Although it has been nearly 30 years since the first commercial cellular-phone network was launched, advertisers have yet to figure out how to get their messages out to mobile-phone users in a big way. There are 2.2 billion cell-phone subscribers worldwide, a total that is growing by about 25% each year, according to the Mobile Marketing Association (MMA). Yet spending on ads carried over cellular networks last year amounted to just $1.5 billion worldwide, a fraction of the $424 billion global ad market.

But as the number of eyeballs glued to tiny screens multiplies, so does the mobile handset's value as a pocket billboard. Consumers are increasingly using their phones for things other than voice calls, such as text messaging, downloading songs and games, and accessing the Internet. By 2010, 70 million Asians are expected to be watching videos and TV programs on handsets. All of these activities give advertisers fresh options for reaching audiences. During soccer's World Cup last summer, for example, Adidas used real-time scores, highlight reels and games to lure thousands of fans to a website set up for mobile-phone access. "Our target audience was males ages 17 to 25," says Marcus Spurrell, Adidas regional new-media manager for Asia. "Their mobiles are always on, always in their pocket—you just can't ignore [cell phones] as an advertising tool." Says Geoffrey Handley, director of new business for the Hyperfactory, a Shanghai-based ad agency focused on handsets: mobile-phone marketing "has become as vital a platform as TV, online or print."

Not yet, perhaps, but corporate spending on handset advertising is expected to soar to $13.9 billion by 2011, according to marketing-research firm eMarketer. The field got a boost on March 27, when Yahoo! became the first major Internet firm to introduce a mobile-ad network, a service that allows companies to more easily place text, display and video ads on mobile-phone websites in 19 countries. Also leading the way are blue-chip brands including BMW, McDonald's and Proctor & Gamble, companies that are experimenting with mobile-marketing campaigns to find cost-effective ways to tap the medium. When BMW launched new models in China last year, it tried mobile-video ads as well as downloadable screen "wallpaper" and ringtones. "The click-through rates were unbelievable," says BMW marketing manager Alan Yang. "It's the most effective brand-building tool we've tried." To promote its bB minivan in Japan, Toyota offered concert tickets to those who took snapshots of the vehicle with camera phones. For the World Cup, Adidas fielded a game that allowed players to pimp digital sneakers on their handsets.

Advertisers say mobile-phone marketing allows them to target customers efficiently because cellular carriers know who their subscribers are. And as Yang of BMW notes, consumers appear to be receptive. When Johnson & Johnson recently introduced a new contact-lens line in China, it sent an "m-coupon", good for free samples, to tens of thousands of young, urban women via text messages. Nearly 10% of recipients redeemed their coupons by showing the message to store clerks. That's a far higher response rate than the average 0.2% rate for e-mail ads, says David Turchetti, head of the Shanghai-based mobile-marketing firm 21 Communications. Turchetti says more then 9 out of 10 people open and read unsolicited text messages. "With e-mail ads, you're lucky if 20% do so," he says.

Still, the industry faces a host of technical obstacles. Handset technology, network bandwidth and even screen sizes differ among phone manufacturers, countries and carriers, so campaigns must be tailored to individual markets. "It is virtually impossible for a brand or its agency to make a cross-carrier media buy for mobile," says eMarketer senior analyst John du Pre Gauntt. "Brands, agencies and carriers will need to cooperate or risk losing out on one of the world's most prevalent interactive platforms."

The biggest barrier may turn out to be consumers, who could become hostile if their personal phones are suddenly barraged with pitches. Neatly four out of five Americans surveyed by market-research firm Forrester Research last year said they found the idea of ads on their handsets "annoying". Network operators, wary of getting caught up in spam wars like those that plague the Internet, say they're concerned about keeping subscribers happy. "Unwanted or unsolicited text-message spam to our customers' handsets is unacceptable," said Steve Zipperstein, a Verizon Wireless spokesman, after the US carrier in February successfully sued tour company Passport Holidays for spamming. The US, Singapore, India and China are just a few of the countries now considering regulating such communications. "People won't invite you into their pocket unless you offer them value," says Sandy Agarwal, managing director for Asia at mobile-marketing firm Enpocket.

Ultimately, though, the advertising opportunities may prove too tempting to wait for invitations. "Korean teenagers send on average 66 text messages a day," Spurrell says.

"They have a higher emotional attachment to their mobile than to their mother." Now he has to convince consumers to love the ads as much as they love their phones.

Words & Expressions

spam	n.	unwanted e-mail (usually of a commercial nature sent out in bulk)
home in (on sth.)		be directed or move towards sth.
lure	vt.	to attract or tempt (a person or an animal)
blue-chip	n./adj.	(commerce) (industrial share) considered to be a safe investment
tap	vt.	to obtain or make use of sth.
field	vt.	to put into operation
pimp	vt.	to take advantage of
redeem	vt.	to turn in (coupons, for example) and receive something in exchange
unsolicited	adj.	given or sent voluntarily; not asked for
bandwidth	n.	a data transmission rate; the maximum amount of information (bits/second) that can be transmitted along a channel
prevalent	adj.	widely or commonly occurring, existing, accepted, or practiced
barrage	vt.	to bombard with
wary	adj.	marked by keen caution and watchful prudence

Comprehension

1. How did some blue-chip brands market their products through handset advertising? Try to give some detailed examples.
2. Do you think that mobile phone marketing is more effective than other marketing means such as TV commercials and e-mail ads? And what are your reasons?
3. Are there any obstacles this industry is still facing? If so, what are they?
4. Do people feel the idea of ads on their handsets "annoying"? How about you?
5. What is behind the statement "people won't invite you into their pocket unless you offer them value"?

Translation

Please translate the parts in waves into Chinese.

Questions for Discussion
1. What are your ideas about the future of mobile-phone marketing?
2. Do you have a high emotional attachment to your mobile? How about people around you? What kind of view do you hold towards such a phenomenon?

Google Gooses Big Media

Justin Fox

The search giant rewrote the rules of distribution and selling ads. The big movie, TV and print outfits may never catch up.

"CONTENT IS KING." It's a phrase uttered repeatedly by media executives making the case that the movies, music, TV shows, books and journalism their companies produce are the core of their business.

It happens to be a dubious claim. Sure, movies, music and TV shows have value—as do, I feel compelled to add, magazine columns. But they alone have never generated the huge, reliable profits that keep investors happy and pay for midtown-Manhattan skyscrapers. No, the big money in media has always been in distribution.

Sometimes the media companies do this distributing themselves—think TV networks, or newspapers and their delivery boys. But even when others own the movie theater or the bookstores, big media have long been defined by their ability to make sure their products are displayed prominently there. "The historical media play," says consultant John Hagel, "is having privileged access to limited shelf space."

On the Internet, though, the shelves go on and on and on. And as words, music and now video move to this new environment, the traditional economics of media are under attack. Tellingly, the most valuable media company in the world right now is not Disney or News Corp. or Time Warner (owner of Time) but Google, which helps people find stuff on those endless online shelves.

Google makes virtually all its money— $10.6 billion in revenue last year and $3.1 billion in after-tax profit-selling advertisements. But except for a few endeavors like Google Maps, it's a media firm that produces no content. Rather than take on established media outfits as outright competitors, Google has been trying to persuade them to let it help them find audiences and sell ads. Some media powers have signed up. But the prospect of a world organized on Google's terms remains unsettling to executives accustomed to controlling the path their products take to consumers.

"Once, we had a very simple distribution model, our own branded store," Mark Thompson, director general of the British Broadcasting Corporation (BBC), told me. Now "we've got to get used to an environment where people access our content in a variety of different ways." Thompson sees this as an opportunity—the BBC signed a deal in early March to set up three new "channels" on Google's YouTube site to show short video clips from its programs and share in the ad revenue YouTube generates. "One of the things no media organization can do now is canceling the future," he said.

US media giant Viacom—whose founder, Sumner Redstone, is credited with coining the phrase "Content is king"—has taken a different tack. Viacom's *Daily Show* and *Colbert Report* generated a steady stream of popular clips on YouTube. In February the company demanded that YouTube remove the videos, and this month it sues Google for $1 billion. Viacom also signed a deal to distribute shows via YouTube competitor Joost.

Viacom's aim, CEO Philippe Dauman said at an investor conference, was to "show our content in an environment we control." But online audiences gravitate toward neutral platforms that old-line media companies don't control, from Google's search box to Apple's iTunes Music Store—and to YouTube, which already gets more traffic than all the TV-network websites combined, according to research firm Hitwise. "Eventually all of the copyrighted content will be available on virtually all of the sites," Google CEO Eric Schmidt said in an interview on Bloomberg TV. "The growth of YouTube, the growth of online, is so fundamental that these companies are going to be forced to work with and on the Internet."

But will YouTube and sites like it ever deliver media companies the sort of return on content that they're accustomed to? Google's big stroke of money-making genius was to sell ads linked to its search results and sell them to anybody. With five minutes and a credit card, you can sign up to bid on a search phrase—"cream cheese", say—and pay Google only if people actually click through to your site. Google has since extended this advertising network to other sites, so your ads might show up next to a food blogger's post about bagels as well.

For small advertisers and publishers, Google's automated advertising network is a boon: a new, cost-effective way to connect with one another and with customers. But big media companies had already established connections before Google came along, and so far the amounts of money Google offers content producers are paltry compared with what gets thrown around in traditional media. This is especially true with online video, where nobody has really figured out how to match ads to content. YouTube, which Google purchased for $1.65 billion in October, took in just $15 million in revenue last year—less than the cost of making two episodes of the BBC/HBO drama *Rome*.

YouTube's audience is growing fast, and there is a certain inevitability to Schmidt's vision of a world where all content producers succumb to the rules of the Web. Hagel, a veteran at parsing the strategic implications of the Internet for business, thinks established media should be trying to "build relationships with audience members" by recommending content made by others and encouraging participation. He's probably right about this, but lots of purely online companies—among them Yahoo! and, yes, Google—are working on it too. The upshot is that content may increasingly have to stand, or swim, or sink on its own, which isn't something kings do very well.

Words & Expressions

goose	vt.	to poke or pickle in a sensitive part of the body; invigorate; spur into action
outfit	n.	any cohesive unit such as a military company; organization
make the case		prove with facts and reasons
telling	adj.	powerfully persuasive
outright	adj.	complete and clear; without any doubt
sign up		to engage by written agreement
coin	vt.	to make up
tack	n.	a course of action or thought, esp. one that is completely different from a previous one
gravitate	vi.	to be attracted to
blogger	n.	a person who keeps and updates a blog
bagel	n.	a ring-shaped bread
boon	n.	something very helpful or useful
parse	vt.	to analyze syntactically by assigning a constituent structure to (a sentence)

Comprehension

1. What does "Content is king" mean?
2. Why are the traditional economics of media under attack?
3. How can Google become the world's most valuable media company?
4. How does Google sell ads?
5. Do you agree with Hagel's opinion in the last paragraph? And why?

Translation

Please translate the parts in waves into Chinese.

Questions for Discussion

1. Please say what you know about the search giant—Google.
2. What should the rules of distribution and selling ads be in your opinion?

Unit 34

Passage

The Meat and Potatoes of Culture
Robert T. Tuohey

Chinese students majoring in English regularly receive a variety of courses on "foreign culture". Most common are classes outlining British and American culture. Now, anyone who has put some thought into this matter should not only recognize the general importance of this information, but also be able to enumerate the specific goals aimed at.

However, very strange to relate, a large number of teachers, foreign and Chinese, seem to have only the foggiest notion of what they are trying to accomplish in these courses. Most foreign teachers, suddenly confronted with the problem of conveying something of "cultural importance" within 15 brief weeks, opt for the "smorgasbord" approach: Each week a general topic (e.g., holidays) is introduced, a list of key words scrawled across the blackboard, with "activities" (usually amounting to nothing more than conversation) capping the class. The Chinese teachers, however, lacking this general background information, rely instead on force-feeding their students a stale academic diet of "facts and figures" (e.g., population, major cities, and so on). The results of these half-baked ideas, however, are as predictable as unpalatable: the students can't digest a bit of it.

Thus, I deem it high time to scrub out the pan and get the recipe right.

Beyond its simplest, denotative aspect, human language conveys its meaning via implication and connotation. These two elements, by definition, are dependent upon a commonly shared background, which, in the widest sense, is what culture is.

For example, an educated speaker of English might refer to a certain type of poor economic practice as "robbing Peter to pay Paul". Or, again, an American male might remark that there was a "knock out" at his office that he'd asked on a date, but that he "struck out".

Now, unless you are acquainted with the Bible, boxing, and baseball, these examples are all Greek to you.

Let's take an example from Chinese: *ba miao zhu zhang*, meaning to pull on the seedlings to help them to grow. Although this idiom finds an apparently easy equivalent in "haste makes waste", unless in fact you know something of the long struggle China has had in adequately feeding and educating its large population, the saying loses all but its most superficial meaning.

Today, irrevocably, China has assumed its position in the international arena. Ergo, the higher education system in this country has an obligation, not only in regard to its foreign language majors but indeed all its university students, to provide some kind of information about the world at large.

If a university student in China graduates and yet is unable to find France on the map, thinks Plato is a type of dish, and has two words to describe the United States (New York and money), I submit to you that that student is unqualified as a citizen of the modern world.

It's the job of culture classes to prevent this type of blatant ignorance.

Admittedly, this is a challenge, worldwide, for educators. But, then again, as we've certainly managed to incorporate computer literacy into the curriculum, it's not too much to ask that we know a bit about our neighbors.

Putting aside linguistic competence and general world knowledge (which are mere technical matters), we finally arrive at the most important point of cultural studies: an examination of what it means to be human.

Simply put, via the contemplation of the greatest achievements in philosophy, literature and the arts, we approach an understanding of what humanity has been, and could be.

Indeed, how much poorer my world would be without Shakespeare's tragedies, without Laozi's sublime mediations, without Dali's surreal clocks!

Thus, from second-language proficiency to overall knowledge of the world to a deeper understanding of ourselves, individually and collectively, culture classes have a tall order to fill. I like to paraphrase the Latin "Ars longa, Vita brevis" (Art is long, Life is short), for my students as "There's a lot more to this than I can fit into 15 weeks!" The essential point, however, remains valid: I know what I want to convey, have arranged that material into a logical sequence, and do my best to make this information relevant to my students' concerns.

With these goals in mind I can serve up a culture class that is satisfying to both the minds and imaginations of students.

Words & Expressions

enumerate	vt.	to name things on a list one by one
opt for		to choose to take a particular course of action

scrawl	vt.	to write sth. in a careless untidy way, making it difficult to read
cap	vt.	to say or do sth. that is funnier, more impressive, etc. than sth. that has been said or done before
unpalatable	adj.	unpleasant and not easy to accept
blatant	adj.	done in an obvious and open way without caring if people object or are shocked
contemplation	n.	the act of thinking deeply about sth.
sublime	adj.	of very high quality and causing great admiration

Comprehension

1. What do most foreign and Chinese teachers usually do in the course of culture?
2. In which way does foreign language convey its meaning? Give an example.
3. What is "blatant ignorance"?
4. How do you explain "Art is long, life is short"?
5. What are the goals of culture classes?

Translation

Please translate the parts in waves into Chinese.

Questions for Discussion

1. How do you understand the title of this passage?
2. What do you think is the most important when learning culture of foreign countries? And how can one master culture of foreign countries?

Passage

Money Speaks
Liu Jie

Foreign businesspeople are more eager to learn Chinese than ever before, and the booming education industry is cashing in.

Learning Chinese is no longer just fashionable, but is considered a necessity by thousands of aspiring young business people around the world who are keen to jump on the China bandwagon.

Thomas Edwards, a 40-something American expatriate working in Beijing for a US company, studied Chinese before he even landed his present job because he believed his future lay across the Pacific. Now that his future is assured, Edwards continues to sharpen his Chinese whenever he has the chance. At coffee breaks, for example, he makes a point of mixing with his Chinese colleagues to practice his language skills.

"My Chinese has improved a lot in the three months I've been here," he says.

Edwards says that when he started learning Chinese in the United States, it was the popular thing to do. Now learning Chinese has become a huge trend among many young American executives.

The Chinese language craze has spawned a multimillion-dollar business in China. Language schools specializing in teaching non-native speakers have opened in nearly every major city. Thousands of people have quit their jobs to become full-time private Chinese language tutors. Publishing houses are working overtime to churn out education materials and learning aides to teach foreigners Chinese.

The Chinese Language Education Foundation, a non-profit research facility, estimates that there are tens of millions of foreigners around the world studying the Chinese language. Each student, it figures, spends an average of about 1,000 yuan (US $125) on tuition and learning materials every year.

In the past, most foreigners learned Chinese largely because they were fascinated by the country's rich cultural heritage. Now they are studying because they want to do

Business in the fastest growing major economy in the world, says Zhang Li, director of the Business Chinese Department at Peking Language and Culture University (BLCU).

There is, of course, no shortage of Chinese language teachers and teaching facilities in China catering to the increasing numbers of foreign students. Several major universities in Beijing, including BLCU, Peking University and Beijing Foreign Studies University, are offering Chinese language courses to foreign students.

At BLCU, for instance, tuition for a full-time training program ranges from 23,200 yuan (US$2,864) a year for beginners to 28,200 yuan (US$3,841) for advanced students. The university also provides short-term courses at prices ranging from 2,000 yuan (US$247) a month to 10,000 yuan (US$1,235) for three months.

Costs vary greatly, depending on location and facilities. One-on-one lessons can be expensive, with fees ranging from 100 yuan (US$12) to 300 yuan (US$37) per hour.

More multinational companies in China are organizing in-house Chinese language classes for their expatriate employees. Edwards and others say that these classes are designed to help expatriates and their families better understand the cultural background and customs of the local market. Effective communication, Edwards says, is not only about language. It is also about understanding different cultures and ways of thinking.

Zhang says the Chinese language courses at BLCU are designed to meet the needs and requirements of foreign students.

"We emphasize business Chinese because our students are learning the language to find jobs or to help them in negotiations with their Chinese business partners," he says.

Angel Robin, a recent graduate of BLCU, got a job as a sales manager in the Beijing office of a French pharmaceutical company. She makes 6,000 yuan (US$741) a month.

"I think I got the job because I can speak some Chinese," she says.

She says she is happy sharing a two-bedroom apartment with a co-worker and living in Beijing.

"I can feed myself and there is still some money left for me to travel around China," she says. "That's quite enough for me, at least for now."

Robin says one of her British classmates now works as the chief representative of a foreign property-consulting firm's Beijing office. He makes 300,000 yuan (US$37,037) a year, mainly due to his Chinese language skills.

"Speaking the local tongue is a great way to make friends," Edwards says.

"When I greet somebody with the Chinese greeting 'ni hao' I can see the appreciation in their face," Edwards says. "That's a good start, right? The Chinese say we have friends all over the world. I like to say I have teachers all over China."

The proliferation of Chinese language schools throughout the country has prompted the government to take regulatory action, according to Ma Jianfei, deputy director of the China National Office for Teaching Chinese as a Foreign Language. Ma says the purpose is to set standards for Chinese language schools and protect the interests of foreign students.

The office has issued a series of regulations on capital requirements and teaching qualifications. Ma says his bureau is stepping up its supervision by making regular visits to registered schools and evaluating teachers.

Words & Expressions

cash in		to take advantage (of) or profit (from)
expatriate	n.	sb. who does not live in their own country
land	vt.	to get or achieve sth. good, especially in a way which seems easy or unexpected
spawn	vt.	to engender; result in
churn out		to produce something at a fast rate
cater to		to try to satisfy (desires, or needs)
proliferation	n.	a rapid increase in number
prompt	vt.	to give an incentive for action
step up		to speed up; take action

Comprehension

1. What does Thomas Edwards's example try to say?
2. What does the Chinese language craze bring about?
3. Nowadays, why are there so many foreigners learning Chinese? Do their motivations differ from those in the past?
4. Why are multinational companies in China organizing in-house Chinese language classes for their expatriate employees?
5. Is it necessary for government to take regulatory actions to supervise Chinese language schools? And why?

Translation

Please translate the parts in waves into Chinese.

Questions for Discussion

1. What do you think of the Chinese language craze?
2. Since so many foreigners are learning Chinese in order to find a job in China, do you think this will pose a great challenge to us Chinese job-hunters?

Passage

Competitive Travel
Xu Xiaoyan

JALPAK International China Co., Ltd. (JALPAKICC) reached a milestone on December 2, 2003, when it became the first solely foreign-owned tourist company in the Chinese mainland. Established with registered capital of RMB 5 million by JALPAK, a company that handles overseas tourist business for Japan Airline Corp., it serves as an agency that organizes China tours from Japan.

It was the first foreign tourist company that gained approval to set up shop in the Chinese mainland after the Provisional Regulations on the Establishment of Foreign-controlled or Solely Foreign-owned Travel Agencies, jointly issued by the China National Tourism Administration and the Ministry of Commerce, came into effect on July 12 that year.

Under China's WTO commitments, the country was obliged to open its tourism market to foreign competition on December 31, 2005. JALPAKICC therefore beat the rush by an impressive two years. And since the market was thrown open, a host of international travel giants have entered China, such as Gulliver's Travel Associates, Star Cruises, and Business Travel International (BTI). This characteristic stems on one hand from the capabilities of the world's largest tourism companies, and on the other from the fact that China's current policies bar entry to lesser players. According to the Provisional Regulations, entrants must earn annual revenues exceeding US $40 million (for those applying to set up foreign-controlled travel agencies) or US $500 million (for solely foreign-owned travel agencies).

Foreign-funded travel agencies play to their particular strengths in China. For instance, All Nippon Airways Travel Services utilizes its superiority in air transport in organizing Japanese tour groups to China, while Gulliver's Travels focuses on using its advanced network system to provide tourists more conveniences for hotel reservation, ticket purchasing, itinerary arrangement, and tourism facility information checking, by gradually installing its machine terminals in major public places such as airports, train stations, metro stations and so on. Star Cruises runs a cruise service and offers water-based tours, while BTI Jinjiang China aims for top-end holiday consumers.

Under the terms negotiated for WTO entry, outbound travel is still off limits to foreign agents. But that is set to change, and when it does, Chinese tourism companies need to be ready to handle the competition.

Even domestically, some foreign-funded tour operators are grabbing Chinese customers by offering better services and new patterns of consumption. The Australia-based Sai Tourist Group has devised the "Jewish Culture Experience" in the northeast city of Harbin. Gulliver's Travel Associates has meanwhile launched online booking and payments services specially designed for Chinese customers. They can now book with more than 19,000 contracted hotels and various travel routes with their individual travel or business visa to Europe.

Their abundant capital, deep information channels, and advanced operation systems accumulated after years of experience are the three main reasons why Chinese travel agents should fear their foreign competitors—at least for the moment. They have vast, effective Internet-based information systems that allow tourists to book and check routes, ticket prices, hotels and other services at easy conveniences.

This means domestic tour operators will have to shape up in order to compete. They'll have to reconsider their management strategies to match their foreign competitors, and provide clients with a vastly improved, friendly service. Otherwise the country's potential tourist market of 1.3 billion could choose foreign agencies. The experience they get in this regard may also be of use when the outbound market is eventually opened up to foreign competition. In any case, it's good news for Chinese consumers. Competition between domestic and foreign travel agents will lead to far greater choices, much better services, and, of course, reductions in holiday prices. Now then, who's going on vacation?

Words & Expressions

milestone	n.	(fig.) a very important stage or event; a turning point
provisional	adj.	under terms not final or fully worked out or agreed upon
come into effect		(esp. of laws, rules, etc.) to reach the stage of being in use
commitment	n.	things one has promised to do; pledge; undertaking
bar	vt.	to obstruct (sth.) so as to prevent progress
lesser	adj.	smaller in amount, value, or importance, especially in a comparison between two things
itinerary	n.	a route or proposed route of a journey
outbound	adj.	travelling away from a particular point; (going) far away, esp. to another country

off limits		(of a place) not to be entered or visited (by sb.)
operator	n.	the owner or manager of a business or an industrial enterprise
devise	vt.	to form, plan, or arrange in the mind; design or contrive
shape up		to develop in a certain way

Comprehension

1. Why does the author think that the JALPAKICC reached a milestone on December 2, 2003?
2. How does the author illustrate the phenomenon that only a host of international travel giants have entered China?
3. Should Chinese travel agents fear their foreign competitors?
4. What should domestic tour operators do to meet the challenge from foreign competitors?
5. How do you interpret the title "Competitive Travel"? Which party do you think is enjoying competitiveness presently, the Chinese travel agencies or the foreign ones?

Translation

Please translate the parts in waves into Chinese.

Questions for Discussion

1. Will the competition between domestic and foreign travel agents benefit consumers?
2. Do you think Chinese tourism companies can handle the competition after its tourism market is fully opened to foreign competition?

Vocabulary

A

abet vt.	4
accessory n.	22
account for	15
accountability n.	24
accrue vi.	26
adduce vt.	26
adjunct n.	1
adverse adj.	14
aftermath n.	13
akin adj.	23
alliance n.	2
amity n.	11
annals n.	28
appreciate vi.	20
arrest vt.	10
assume vt.	15
ascendancy n.	10
assembly n.	23
assess vt.	9
autarky n.	16

B

backdrop n.	11
backlash n.	6
backup n.	31
bagel n.	33
ballooning market	30
bandwidth n.	32
bankruptcy n.	30
bar vt.	36
barrage vt.	32
barter vt.	5
beef up	5
benchmark vt.	22
binding adj.	12
blackout n.	31
blatant adj.	34
blogger n.	33
blue-chip n. /adj.	32
bolster vt.	4
bolt vt.	27
boom n.	15
boon n.	33
breakneck adj.	18
bring ... under control	10
buffer n.	4
bulwark n.	11
buoyancy n.	13
buy on credit	3
buyout n.	8

C

cap vt.	34
capital account	25
capital supply	30
capture vt.	1
cash in	35
cash out	8
catalyst n.	28
catastrophe n.	18
catch up with	6
catchy adj.	2

cater to	35	decouple *vt.*	16
caveat *n.*	5	deliberative *adj.*	23
certification *n.*	19	delve *vi.*	30
charisma *n.*	27	demagoguery *n.*	16
charter *vt.*	24	demonstration program	19
chink *n.*	31	denominator *n.*	12
churn out	35	deploy *vt.*	22
coin *vt.*	33	depository *n.*	24
collaboration *n.*	23	derivative *adj.*	30
collateral *adj.*	7	deregulation *n.*	6
come into effect	36	desertification *n.*	18
commitment *n.*	36	deterioration *n.*	14
compatible *adj.*	27	deviation *n.*	26
compliance *n.*	27	devise *vt.*	36
component *n.*	9	devour *vt.*	15
confederation *n.*	9	diagonal *n.*	2
constituency *n.*	23	dictate *vt.*	17
constitute *vt.*	17	directing *n.*	9
contemplation *n.*	34	disentangle *vt.*	26
contractionary *adj.*	14	dismantle *vt.*	19
controlling *n.*	9	disparity *n.*	11
convergence *n.*	12	dissemination *n.*	7
convert *vt.*	3	divestiture *n.*	8
convert *vt.*	17	document *vt.*	24
counterpart *n.*	29	downturn *n.*	14
covariance *n.*	24	draw upon	9
credit authorization	20	drive ... up	14
credit policy	3	dynamic *n.*	12
cumbersome *adj.*	16	dynamics *n.*	14
curriculum vitae	1		
current account	25		

D

E

		earmark *vt.*	13
curtail *vt.*	16	ease *vt.*	29
cutthroat *adj.*	30	economize *vt.*	17
		elimination *n.*	1
dampen *vt.*	24	embed *vt.*	24
de facto	25	enact *vt.*	4
debilitating *adj.*	25	encompass *vt.*	28
decelerate *vi.*	10	engender *vt.*	24

engineer *vt.*	10
enshrine *vt.*	12
enumerate *vt.*	34
envisage *vt.*	23
espouse *vt.*	23
European Community	12
exacerbate *vt.*	14
exogenous *adj.*	16
expansionary *adj.*	14
expatriate *n.*	35
exponentially *adv.*	1
exposure *n.*	24

F

facilitate *vt.*	29
facilitator *n.*	12
fad *n.*	8
fashion *vt.*	9
field *vt.*	32
financial instrument	25
fledgling *adj.*	28
flotilla *n.*	31
fluctuation *n.*	13
forex	20
forge *vt.*	29
forwards *n.*	20
frenzied *adj.*	4
friction *n.*	7
frugality *n.*	17

G

gallop *vi.*	16
generate *vt.*	28
go public	28
go up against	29
goose *vt.*	33
gravitate *vi.*	33

H

hallmark *n.*	23
halt *vt.*	7
hamper *vt.*	25
hard-core *adj.*	16
hazy *adj.*	22
hedging *n.*	20
heft *n.*	4
hike *n.*	13
hoard *vt.*	22
hold ... back	9
home in (on sth.)	32
homogeneity *n.*	12
honor *vt.*	3
hunch *vt.*	29
hurdle *n.*	5
hydraulic *adj.*	17
hydroelectricity *n.*	18

I

implant *vt.*	8
in excess of	10
in tandem (with)	18
incendiary *adj.*	7
inception *n.*	19
incremental *adj.*	22
incur *vt.*	3
indicator *n.*	17
infighting *n.*	8
inflated *adj.*	8
inflation *n.*	13
inflationary *adj.*	13
institute *vt.*	23
integrate *vt.*	28
interface *vi.*	27
inventory *n.*	3
iron out	31
isolationism *n.*	7

itinerary n. 36

J

jeopardize vt. 26
joint venture 30
jump on 6
jurisdiction n. 25

K

keep on one's toes 9

L

lackluster adj. 6
land vt. 35
lax adj. 5
leapfrog vt. 22
legion n. 11
lesser adj. 36
leverage vt. 28
liberalization n. 25
liquidity n. 21
lure vt. 32
luster n. 9

M

magnify vt. 14
make the case 33
malicious adj. 7
malignant adj. 25
malleable adj. 22
management n. 9
mangle vt. 16
manipulate vt. 26
mayhem n. 16
mediocre adj. 8
melee n. 16
meltdown n. 31
meritocratic adj. 22
milestone n. 36

misgiving n. 4
misperception n. 11
misstep n. 4
mitigate vt. 4
mogul n. 30
monitoring n. 9
mop up 21
morose adj. 16
motivate vt. 24
mounting adj. 4
mull vt. 16

N

netizen n. 30
notwithstanding prep. 11
nuanced adj. 11

O

obsolete adj. 28
off limits 36
offset vt. 14
offshore adj. 21
onerous adj. 4
ongoing adj. 10
online game 30
operator n. 36
opt for 34
organizing n. 9
outbound adj. 36
outfit n. 33
outlay n. 3
outpace vt. 21
outright adj. 33
outsize adj. 10
outweigh vt. 14
overarching adj. 11
overcapacity n. 21
overhead adj. 27
overlap n. 24

| overshoot | vi. | 25 |

P

paltry	adj.	29
paraphernalia	n.	28
parity	n.	20
parse	vt.	33
paucity	n.	26
payroll	n.	27
penchant	n.	11
peripheral	adj.	23
perpetuate	vt.	22
perquisite	n.	26
pertain	vi.	26
pimp	vt.	32
pitch	n.	1
pitfall	n.	1
plague	vt.	23
planning	n.	9
pledge	vt.	21
pluralize	vt.	17
polystyrene	n.	18
pool	vt.	12
portfolio	n.	24
pose	vt.	29
position	n.	20
post mortem		25
postulate	vt.	23
premium	n.	6
prevalent	adj.	32
price bidding		20
prodigious	adj.	11
product line		28
proffer	vt.	6
profligate	adj.	16
project	vt.	3
project	vt.	21
projection	n.	15
proliferation	n.	35
prompt	vt.	35
promulgate	vt.	24
propel	vt.	19
propitious	adj.	11
proposition	n.	1
prosper	vi.	23
protectionism	n.	7
proverbial	adj.	6
provisional	adj.	36
proxy	n.	26
prudent	adj.	21

Q

QDII	(abbr.)	25
QFII	(abbr.)	25
quantitative	adj.	17
quantum leap		22
quench	vt.	5

R

rake in		29
rampant	adj.	8
rating agency		25
recession	n.	14
recoup	vt.	7
recycling	n.	19
redeem	vt.	32
regress	vi.	22
remedy	vt.	18
render	vt.	28
renewable resources		19
repercussion	n.	16
reside	vi.	1
resurgence	n.	5
retailing channel		28
retention	n.	2
reverberation	n.	5
review	vt.	7
revision	n.	13

Vocabulary

rig *vt.*	7	
rule out	31	
rupture *vt.*	31	

S

sanction *n.*	12
save *prep.*	31
scalability *n.*	2
scenario *n.*	2
scramble *vi.*	15
scrawl *vt.*	34
screed *n.*	11
sequence *vt.*	13
shake-up *n.*	11
shape *vt.*	15
shape up	36
shoddy *adj.*	6
sign up	33
skirmish *n.*	16
spam *n.*	32
sparkle *vt.*	16
spate *n.*	16
spawn *vt.*	11
speculative *adj.*	21
spell out	7
spinoff *n.*	8
spot market	20
spurt *n.*	5
staggering *adj.*	27
staid *adj.*	28
stake *n.*	28
stall *vt.*	7
stark *adj.*	6
start-up *n.*	1
step up	35
stoke up	14
strata *n.*	11
stringent *adj.*	25
subdue *vt.*	13

subjugation *n.*	11
sublime *adj.*	34
subsidy *n.*	14
substitute *n.*	2
surveillance *n.*	13
sustainability *n.*	15
swaps *n.*	20
synergistic *adj.*	11

T

tab *n.*	26
tacit *adj.*	27
tack *n.*	33
take the helm of	9
tap *vt.*	17
tap *vt.*	32
teething problems	19
telling *adj.*	33
temblor *n.*	31
temper *vt.*	11
template *n.*	1
the status quo	22
thrust *n.*	11
tie up	3
toe the line	8
trade-off *n.*	24
trauma *n.*	11
tread *vi.*	17
tried-and-true *adj.*	28
turnaround	13

U

underestimate *vt.*	2
underscore *vt.*	10
unpalatable *adj.*	34
unsolicited *adj.*	32
upstart *n.*	5
upstart *adj.*	28
uptick *n.*	16

V

venture *vi.*		18
versatility *n.*		25
vet *vt.*		5
virtual gear		30
voracious *adj.*		10

W

wary *adj.*		32
weed ... out		15
weighted average		20
wire service		7
withstand *vt.*		17
working capital		3
wreak *vt.*		18

Bibliography

Argenti, Paul A. & Foreman, Janis. The communication advantage [A]. In Crainer, Stuart & Dearlove, Des(eds), *Financial Times Handbook of Management* [C]. London: Pearson Education Limited, 2001: 292-296.

Elegant, Simon. China's unwelcome mat [N]. *Time*, 25 September 2006.

Erickson, Jim. Hanging by a thread [N]. *Time*. 15 January 2007.

Feng, Jie. Money supply target lowered [N]. *China Daily*, 6 January 2006.

Fox, Justin. Google gooses big media [N]. *Time*, 26 March 2007.

Griffin, Ricky W. & Ebert, Ronald J. *Business* [M]. 6th ed. London: Pearson Education Limited, 2002.

Joffe, Josef. Those gloating dismal scientists [N]. *Time*, 29 January 2007.

Kim, W. Chan & Mauborgne, Renee. Strategy in the knowledge economy [A]. In Crainer, Stuart & Dearlove, Des (eds), *Financial Times Handbook of Management* [C]. London: Pearson Education Limited, 2001: 280-284.

Kingsbury, Kathleen. Spam, to go [N]. *Time*, 9 April 2007.

Kuhn, Robert Lawrence. Changes and challenges [N]. *China Daily*, 15 November 2005.

Li, Qian. To be a well-off Witkey? [J]. *China Today*, February 2007: 32.

Li, Weitao. Shattered faith [J]. *China Daily Business Weekly*, March 2006: 13-19.

Liu, Jie. Money speaks [J]. *China Daily Business Weekly*, March 2006: 13-19.

Liu, Yunyun. Virtual world, real fortune [J]. *Beijing Review*, March 2007: 34-35.

Maughan, Lance. Waste not want not [J]. *China Today*, August 2006: 36.

Mullins, Richard. Green or gray? [J]. *China Today*, November 2006: 42.

Rajan, Raghuram. Balancing act [N]. *Time*, 25 September 2006.

Santomero, Anthony M. The revolution in risk management [A]. In Crainer, Stuart & Dearlove, Des (eds), *Financial Times Handbook of Management* [C]. London: Pearson Education Limited, 2001: 488-492.

Scase, Richard. Work beyond 2010 [A]. In Crainer, Stuart & Dearlove, Des(eds), *Financial Times Handbook of Management* [C]. London: Pearson Education Limited, 2001: 132-137.

Shulman, Joel. The key challenges facing corporate america at present [J]. *Global Business Review*, 2004(7): 58.

Smith, Adam. A sharp AIM [N]. *Time*, 8 April 2007.

Tabet, Joe & Angehrn, Albert. *Financial Times Mastering Management 2.0: Your*

Single-source Guide to Becoming a Master of Management [M]. London: Prentice Hall, 2001.

Tuohey, Robert T. The meat and potatoes of culture [J]. *Beijing Review*, March 2007: 48.

Xu, Xiaoyan. Competitive travel [J]. *China Today*, April 2007: 42.

Zhang, Dingmin. Forex rate forming mechanism reformed [N]. *China Daily*, 4 January 2006.

Zhang, Kuo. Recycling big [J]. *China Today*, October 2006: 78-79.

Zhou, Dadi. Five steps to prevent future energy woes [N]. *China Daily*, 16 November 2005.

Zingales, Luigi. The value of being in control [A]. In Crainer, Stuart & Dearlove, Des (eds), *Financial Times Handbook of Management* [C]. London: Pearson Education Limited, 2001: 482-487.